D0940059

Alabama

Daily Devotions For Die-Hard Kids

Crimson Tide

TO PARENTS/GUARDIANS FROM THE AUTHOR

DAILY DEVOTIONS FOR DIE-HARD KIDS is an adaptation of our DAILY DEVOTIONS FOR DIE-HARD FANS series. It is suggested for children ages 6 to 12, but that guideline is, of course, flexible. Only the parents or an adult can appraise the spiritual maturity of their children.

The devotions are written with the idea that a parent or adult will join the children to act as a mentor and spiritual guide for each devotion and the discussion that may ensue. The devotions seek to engage the child by capitalizing on his or her interest in the particular collegiate team the family follows. The interest in college sports is thus an oblique and somewhat tricky way, if you will, to lead your children to reading the Bible and learning about God, Jesus, and faith.

Each devotion contains a short Bible reading (except for occasional longer stories that must be read in their entirety), a paraphrase of the pertinent scripture verse(s), a true Crimson Tide sports story, and a theological discussion that ties everything together behind a common theme. The devotion then concludes with a suggested activity that is based on the theme of the day. I link each day's theological message to a child's life by referring to school, household chores, video games, relations with parents and teachers, etc.

The devotions are intended to be fun for both the adult and the child, but they are also intended to be attempts to spark interest in quite serious matters of faith and living a godly life. A point of emphasis throughout the book is to impress upon the child that faith is not just for the times when the family gathers for formal worship in a particular structure, but rather is for every moment of every day wherever he or she may be.

Our children are under attack by the secular world as never before. It is a time fraught with danger for the innocence and the faith of our most precious family members. I pray that this book will provide your children with a better understanding of what it means to be a Christian. I also pray that this book will help lay the foundation for what will be a lifelong journey of faith for your children. May God bless you and your family.

ED MCMINN

Crimson Tide

Daily Devotions for Die-Hard Kids: Alabama Crimson Tide

Manufactured in the United States of America.

Cover design by John Powell and Slynn McMinn;
Interior design by Slynn McMinn

DAILY DEVOTIONS FOR DIE-HARD FANS

ACC
CLEMSON TIGERS
DUKE BLUE DEVILS
FSU SEMINOLES
GA. TECH YELLOW JACKETS
NORTH CAROLINA TAR HEELS
NC STATE WOLFPACK
VIRGINIA CAVALIERS
VIRGINIA TECH HOKIES

BIG 12
BAYLOR BEARS
OKLAHOMA SOONERS
OKLAHOMA STATE COWBOYS
TCU HORNED FROGS
TEXAS LONGHORNS
TEXAS TECH RED RAIDERS

BIG 10
MICHIGAN WOLVERINES
OHIO STATE BUCKEYES
PENN STATE NITTANY LIONS

SEC
ALABAMA CRIMSON TIDE
ARKANSAS RAZORBACKS
AUBURN TIGERS
MORE AUBURN TIGERS
FLORIDA GATORS
GEORGIA BULLDOGS
MORE GEORGIA BULLDOGS
KENTUCKY WILDCATS
LSU TIGERS
MISSISSIPPI STATE BULLDOGS
MISSOURI TIGERS
OLE MISS REBELS
SOUTH CAROLINA GAMECOCKS
MORE S. CAROLINA GAMECOCKS
TEXAS A&M AGGIES
TENNESSEE VOLUNTEERS

NASCAR

DAILY DEVOTIONS FOR DIE-HARD KIDS

ALABAMA CRIMSON TIDE; AUBURN TIGERS; GEORGIA BULLDOGS

GOOD OLD DAYS

Read Psalm 102:1-5.

Lord, my days disappear like smoke.

Imagine this: One time in a game, the Tide football players got attacked by some fans with umbrellas and walking canes!

A long time ago football was a lot different. Alabama's first game was way back in 1892. People didn't even have cars then! The Tide won that first-ever game 56-0 against a high school team. Just think about Alabama playing your high school in football.

In those days, the fans could get onto the field during a game. In one game against Ole Miss in the late 1890s, an Alabama player fell on one of their guys hard with his knee. The Ole Miss fans didn't like it one bit. They ran out of the stands and hit the Alabama player with walking canes and umbrellas and anything else they could grab hold of.

Crimson Tide

The game was a lot rougher back then, too. One player said, "In those days, football wasn't a lady's game." One team Bama played in 1899 had pro boxers and guys who worked on ships on their team. They surely didn't have college students playing. A Tide player said they kicked him and bit him. When the game was over, he had two black eyes, a swollen nose, and a bad limp.

Bama football isn't like that today because time does not stand still. That means things change. When they do, you have memories, things you remember. What grade are you in now? Remember last year and some of the things you did? Remember your baptism?

You will always have those memories. God is always with you, too. Today may be one of those good old days you will remember someday, but you must share it with God. A true "good old day" is one God is a part of.

Make list of things you can do to make God a part of your day (like saying a blessing). Try to do them all.

DYNASTY

Read 2 Samuel 7:12-17.

David's kingdom will never end.

After Alabama beat the daylights out of Notre Dame for the 2012 national title, a lot of folks said Alabama was a "dynasty."

A dynasty happens when someone is in first place or beats everybody else for a long time. To be a dynasty in college football is to be number one for several seasons.

When Alabama beat Notre Dame 42-14, it was the Tide's second straight national title and third in four seasons. They didn't just win; they slaughtered the Fighting Irish. An *ESPN* announcer said Alabama was so good they should get a trophy and a half. That same TV person said what Alabama had done in winning the three titles was so good and so unusual that it made history.

Alabama head coach Nick Saban would have

none of this dynasty talk. He said he wasn't really interested in words like "dynasty." Instead, he said, he just wanted his team to do its best. If it happened that they were the best year after year, that's just the way it is.

But there's no doubt what Alabama has done in college football: It has set up a dynasty.

As much as you want them to, Alabama can't win every SEC title or every national title. The Tide even lost two games in the 2013 season.

Have you ever noticed that your life is like a football season? You win some and lose some. You may be so good at something like a video game or spelling that you almost never lose or make mistakes. But you do sometimes.

Only one dynasty will never end. That's the one God set up with King David a long time ago, even before football. God promised David a king to set up God's kingdom.

That king is Jesus; his kingdom lasts forever.

Name something you're really good at, so good that you're like a dynasty. Then tell about the last time you lost at it.

BAD WEATHER

Read Nahum 1:3-5.

God alone controls the wind and the storms.

A basketball shot once helped save lives.

In the SEC Tournament in 2008 in Atlanta, Alabama was behind Mississippi State by three points with just two seconds left in the game. Bama guard Mykal Riley prayed, "Lord, please let me hit this shot" when he shot just as the buzzer went off. His prayer was answered. The shot was good, but it did much more than just tie up a basketball game.

During the extra time, the crowd suddenly heard a big roar. Some of the material from the roof floated onto the court. Some metal fell also. A tornado had just passed by the building! It flipped cars over like toys, damaged the roof, and knocked over light towers.

But all 14,825 folks in the building were safe

because they were inside watching the game. If Mykal Riley had missed his shot, the game would have ended. Many of the people would have been walking back to their hotel rooms just as the tornado hit. They would have been walking right in the path of the storm!

Ever since then, Mykal Riley's basket has been known as "The Shot That Saved Lives."

You can look out a window and see a storm coming, but you can't stop it, can you? You can do a lot of things, but only God controls the weather.

God has so much power you can't imagine it. But you also can't imagine just how much God loves you. He loves you so much that as Jesus he died in pain on a nasty cross for you.

God is so powerful that he can make it rain and can push the clouds around. The weather does what God tells it to. But the strongest thing of all about God is his love for you.

List all the kinds of bad weather you can think of. Tell a parent what you'd do in case of each one.

SMART MOVE

Read 1 Kings 4:29-31; 11:4.

Solomon was wise until he grew old and didn't follow God with all his heart anymore.

It sure didn't look like Alabama softball coach Patrick Murphy was making a smart move.

In the 2009 softball college world series, the Tide trailed Arizona State 2-0 in the fourth inning. Alabama loaded the bases with two outs. Brittany Rogers was the next batter.

That was perfect for the Tide. She is one of the greatest players in Bama softball history. She was four times an All-America, meaning she was the best player in the country at her position. She could hit; her batting average of .417 is the second-highest in the history of Alabama softball.

So what did Coach Murphy do? He didn't let Brittany bat! Instead, he sent a freshman up to bat. It was Jazlyn Lunceford, who hadn't batted in two weeks! She hadn't had a base hit in 38 days, over a month.

Was that a smart move?

It must have been. Jazlyn hit a grand slam home run and Alabama won 6-2.

Remember that time you left your homework lying on your desk at home? That cold morning you went to school without a jacket? The time your library book was overdue?

Just because we make good grades in school doesn't mean we don't do some dumb things now and then. Plenty of smart people sometimes say and do things that aren't too smart. Like Solomon when he got old.

Some people even say that if you're really smart you can't believe in God. How dumb is that? Who do they think made us smart in the first place?

You got your brains and your smarts from God. Forgetting that isn't smart at all.

Talk about why it's smart to love God and follow Jesus.

UNEXPECTEDLY

Read Luke 2:1-7.

Mary gave birth to her first child. It was a boy she named Jesus.

Texas tried something nobody was expecting, but it helped Bama win a championship.

In the Rose Bowl on Jan. 7, 2010, Alabama led 17-6 with only 29 seconds left in the first half. Everybody expected the Longhorns not to run a play; they would just let those 29 seconds tick off the clock. Then they could go to the locker room to see if they could come up with a way to stop Alabama.

But that's not what they did. Instead, Texas tried to catch Alabama by surprise; the Longhorns threw a little short pass. But Alabama lineman Marcell Dareus was expecting it. He tipped the ball and then caught it. After that, he ran 28 yards for a touchdown.

Nobody expected it but Bama suddenly led

Crimson Tide

24-6. Unexpectedly, the game was pretty much over because Texas was so far behind. The Tide went on to beat Texas 37-21 and win the 2009 national title.

Something is unexpected when you didn't know it was going to happen. It can be good or bad. Maybe you had a field trip planned at school and you woke up sick and couldn't go. Or you found a dollar bill on the sidewalk. Life surprises us a lot.

God is just like that. He surprises us so we can remember that he's still around. Like the time he was born as the baby Jesus.

There is nothing that God can't do in your life. The only thing that holds God back is when you don't believe he can do something. Or when you don't live each day with God in your heart and on your mind.

You should always be ready for God to do something unexpected in your life.

Tell about a time you expected one thing and got something completely different. Was it a good or a bad surprise?

FAILURE

Read Luke 22:54-62.

A girl said Peter was with Jesus. He answered, "I don't know him."

Wallace Wade won so many games at first that some folks called him a failure later.

Coach Wade was the first truly great Alabama head football coach. In 1925, he made history. That's when the unbeaten Crimson Tide became the first team from the South to play in the Rose Bowl.

Nobody figured Bama had a chance against the Washington Huskies. That's because most folks thought Southern football was no good. Can you believe that?

But Alabama didn't fail. The Tide upset the Huskies 20-19 and won Alabama's first-ever national title.

Coach Wade's team the next year also went undefeated and played in the Rose Bowl. That meant Alabama had won 22 straight wins in the regular season.

But three years followed when Bama didn't win as many games. Because Coach Wade had won so many games, many fans thought he was now a failure. He decided to leave.

In his last season, in 1930, his team went 10-0, won the Rose Bowl, and won yet another national title. Coach Wade was no failure!

We all fail at some things in our lives. That means we don't do as well as we expect. Maybe you crashed your bicycle one time when you rode it or didn't win a game at recess.

Failure happens in life. Even Peter failed; he lied and said he had never met Jesus — three times! Yet Jesus picked him to begin the Christian church.

If we believe in Jesus, God always forgives us for failing just as he did Peter. The only failure that is forever is failing to love Jesus.

Think about a time you failed by doing something wrong. Did you ask God to forgive you? If you didn't, do it now.

TOP SECRET

Read Romans 2:1-4, 16.

One day, God will appoint Jesus to judge all the secret thoughts people keep hidden in their hearts.

Tennessee folks once accused Alabama of having a spy at their practices.

In 1954, Tennessee was favored to beat the Tide. Instead, Alabama spanked the Volunteers 27-0. It was the worst beatdown that Bama had laid on UT since way back in 1906.

Tennessee fans looked around for a reason why they had been stomped so badly. They came up with the strange claim that Alabama had spied on their practices. That meant the Tide had learned all their secrets for the game.

In fact, a "spy" had been caught red-handed the week before the game. He was on the hill above Tennessee's practice field. He admitted he was a student at Alabama but denied that

Crimson Tide

he was a spy.

The student said that he had made a bet with some boys back home in Tuscaloosa. He bragged to them that he could get into a UT class. And he did it. He told Tennessee officials that their students were really friendly.

You probably have some secrets you keep from certain people. Do you tell your sister or brother everything? How about your mom and dad? Maybe there's a girl or a boy at school or at church that you really like but you haven't told anyone.

You can keep some secrets from the world. You must never think, though, that you can keep a secret from God. God knows everything: all your mistakes, all your sins, all the bad things you say or think.

But here's something that's not a secret: No matter what God knows about you, he still loves you. Enough to die for you on a cross.

List some secrets you have that you wish God didn't know about. Pray for forgiveness for any of them you need to.

ALL IN

Read Deuteronomy 6:4-9.

Love God with all your heart, with all your soul, with all your strength.

One day at practice, Bear Bryant caught his players totally by surprise. What did he do? He suddenly started singing.

ESPN has called Coach Bryant "simply the best there ever was." He won 323 games as a big-time college football coach. He coached at Alabama from 1958-1982 and won six national championships.

In 1981, Coach Bryant began his 43rd season as a football coach. He was 68 years old and he was an old man. One sportswriter said, "He can look very old sometimes." The writer said Coach Bryant's pants just drooped off his backside like old men's britches do. The Bear just sort of shuffled along. The coach said he took eleven pills every morning.

He even admitted that he got tired of it all sometimes. So why did he keep coaching? "I do love the football," he said. Love drove the Bear to coach even when he was old and tired.

So what song did Coach Bryant sing that morning at practice? It was a hymn called "Love Lifted Me."

You are a true Alabama fan. That means you love the Tide whether they win or lose. You never quit cheering for them.

That's the way you should love God — like the Bear loved football. A long time ago, God told us to love him with all our heart, all our soul, and all our strength. That hasn't changed.

God wants you to love him as hard as you can. All the time. Never stop.

No matter how hard you try, you can never love God more than he loves you. You see, God loves you — with all his heart, all his soul, and all his strength.

Make a list of everybody and everything you love the most, even your pets. Where is God on that list?

WATER POWER

Read Acts 10:44-48.

Peter asked, "Can anyone keep these people from being baptized with water?"

The fans hooted and hollered and went wild. The stands were packed. Somebody even smushed an orange. Alabama-Tennessee football? Nope. Swimming.

Bama and UT were the kings of SEC swimming when they met in February 1978. Alabama had even finished second in the nation the season before.

Both teams had tried some tricks over the years. One time, the Tide head coach put the Vol team next to Bama's spirit band and in front of a drafty doorway. That way it was too noisy for them to talk and too cold when they got out of the pool.

Believe it or not, the Tennessee swimmers

wore coonskin caps that February day. They emptied a bottle of "Big Orange" water into Alabama's pool to make it seem like their home water. The crowd hooted and booed until a Tide student in combat boots stomped on an orange. That turned the hoots to cheers.

Alabama beat Tennessee 63-50. The water that day wasn't orange despite that bottle. It was pure crimson.

Do you like to go swimming? Or take a boat ride? Man, the beach is fun with all that sand and sun and water. Is anything more exciting than a water slide?

Water is fun, but you need it to stay alive. You have to drink water every day.

Water is so important that it is even a part of your faith in Jesus. It's called baptism. A person who is baptized — including you — is marked by the water as someone who belongs to Jesus. It tells the world you are a Christian and that Jesus is your Lord.

Have you been baptized? If so, talk about what it was like. If not, is it time?

CHANGES

Read Romans 6:3-6.

We who were baptized in Christ Jesus change and live a new life.

When Bear Bryant hit town, a lot of things changed. Some folks didn't like it.

Billboards welcomed the new head football coach to Tuscaloosa in 1958. Folks were all excited because Bama football had been bad for three years in a row. They expected some changes; they got them all right.

The coach began laying down the law right away. He told some rich local businessmen they couldn't hang out in his office anymore. They weren't welcome when he was working.

The Bear also told these rich men that he would not be eating long lunches with them anymore. He had too much work to do.

There was more. Coach Bryant told folks they couldn't just walk into Alabama practices

Crimson Tide

like they had been doing. They fussed and said they would come in anyway, so he locked the gates. Boy, were they mad!

But soon they figured out that the coach was making all the changes so Alabama could win more football games. They were all happy after that.

As you grow up, you change. You get taller. You get a different haircut. You get some new friends. Maybe even your family moves into a new house or new town.

But those are all changes on the outside. The biggest change of all is one that comes from inside you, in your heart. That change comes when you meet Jesus.

Jesus doesn't change the way you look. He does change the way you feel. Jesus makes you more loving and happier. He makes you want to help other people. Jesus changes you so you will be more like him.

Name some ways the way you look has changed. Then name some ways Jesus has changed the way you act.

YOU NEVER KNOW

Read Exodus 3:7-12.

Moses asked God, "Who am I to go before Pharaoh?" God answered, "I will be with you."

You never know what you can do until you try. But playing golf when you're blind?

Charley Boswell played football and baseball for Alabama from 1937-39. He was a star half-back on the football team.

During World War II, Captain Boswell saved some lives by pulling several soldiers out of tanks that were on fire. He went back to save someone else, but one of the tanks exploded. He was blinded by the blast.

Boswell was in a hospital in Pennsylvania when a therapist (a person who helps injured people get well) had a crazy idea. He said Boswell ought to give golf a try. "I thought it was a joke," Boswell said. It wasn't.

Crimson Tide

The therapist convinced the former Alabama star he could teach him to play golf. On a golf course, he helped Boswell line up the ball and the way he stood. He drove the ball 200 yards right down the middle of the fairway.

Charley Boswell became a legend, winning 28 blind golf championships and even getting a hole-in-one.

You're like Charley Boswell and Moses. You never know what you can do until you try. You may think you can't play football, cook supper, or run the lawn mower. But have you tried?

Your parents sometimes tell you to do things you think you can't do. God is the same way. You just never know what God is going to ask you to do. Sing a solo in church. Tell someone else about Jesus. Help an old person.

You may think, "I can't do that." But if it's something God wants you to do, you can. You trust him. With God's help, you can do it.

Think of something you've never tried before but would like to do. Decide to do it and pray for God to help you.

PIONEER SPIRIT

Read Luke 5:4-11.

They pulled their boats on shore and left everything to follow Jesus.

How funny would it be if everybody shot a basketball with two hands? Well, everybody did until an Alabama player changed all that.

James "Lindy" Hood played basketball for the Crimson Tide from 1929-1931. He was 6-feet, 7-inches tall, which was real big for back then. Believe it or not, he was too tall for the Alabama gymnasium. It had a balcony around the edges of the court, and one time Lindy jumped up and hit it. He cut a finger and had to miss a game.

But Lindy wasn't just tall. He was so good he was Alabama's first basketball All-America. As a junior in 1930, he led the team to a 20-0 record and the SEC championship. That is still Alabama's only undefeated team ever.

Crimson Tide

It's funny sounding but it's true. You might want to go outside and try it. In Lindy's day, everybody shot the ball with two hands, not with one hand as they do now. But Lindy didn't shoot that way. He was the first player in college basketball to shoot with one hand.

A pioneer is a person, like Lindy Hood, who is the first person to do something or to try something no one else has done before. The disciples who gave up fishing to follow Jesus were pioneers.

Being a pioneer is scary, but it's also fun. Learning something new in school, going to a new place on vacation, riding a new ride at the fair — it's exciting!

God wants you to go to new places and to try new things for him. He wants you to follow him no matter what. After a while, you will get really good at being a Christian and then you can help others become pioneers for Jesus.

On a note card, list some new things you can do for God. Decorate the card and carry it with you all day as a reminder.

NEW STUFF

Read Hebrews 8:6-9.

The new covenant is better than the old one. It has better promises.

Bear Bryant decided it was time for something new because the old stuff just wasn't working anymore.

After the Tide went 6-5 in 1969 and 1970, the head coach had had enough. That just wasn't good enough for Alabama. He needed something new to get Alabama back to winning football games the way it should.

The greatest coach in college football history went to another coach for help! He visited an old friend, Darrell Royal, who was the head coach at Texas. He even moved into the house with Coach Royal and his wife.

Coach Royal ran an offense called the Wishbone. Bear Bryant liked it because it had a lot of running and blocking and not too much

Crimson Tide

passing the football.

The two coaches set up a projector (think DVD player) and watched film of some Texas games. After only one morning, the Bear told Coach Royal to turn it off. He was going to try the Wishbone.

The brand new Alabama offense worked. The Tide went 11-1 in 1971.

There's just nothing like getting new stuff, is there? Like a new bike or video game. Or even new clothes. New things are exciting and fun!

God has given you something new in Jesus. A long time ago, God made some promises to some folks called the Israelites. This set of promises is called a covenant or agreement. But then came Jesus, and God made a new and better covenant that includes everyone, especially you.

It's a new way for you to get to Heaven and live with God and Jesus forever.

Find some stuff in your room that used to be new but is now old. Like Jesus, is the new stuff better?

THANK YOU

Read 1 Thessalonians 5:14-18.

Always give thanks to God no matter what happens to you.

As a Christian, Jay Barker gave thanks no matter what — even when he was benched.

Barker played quarterback for Alabama from 1991 to 1994. He led the Tide to the national title in 1992 and was 35-2-1 as a quarterback.

When Alabama played Georgia in 1994, Barker was not playing well. Head coach Gene Stallings told him to go sit on the bench. How embarrassing was that? Here was a quarterback who had led the team to a national title and he was benched!

But it worked. When Barker went back into the game, he had one of his greatest passing games ever. He threw for 396 yards and the winning touchdown in the 29-28 victory.

Barker shared his faith in Jesus in a television

interview after the game. He even thanked Coach Stallings for putting him on the bench! Barker said the time he spent watching others play fired him up and made him want to play better.

God tells us that we are to give him thanks all the time just as Jay Barker did. Does this mean you should say, "Thank you, God," when you fall down and skin your knee real bad? Or say thanks because your mom is sick?

No, that's silly. God means you are to always look at the good things in your life. You don't give thanks *for* bad things, but you still give thanks *when* bad things happen.

You may feel like God has gone away when some bad things happen, but he hasn't. He's still there, still loving you.

Always thanking God keeps him at the center of your heart and of your life. And that's right where he belongs.

In three minutes on a sheet of paper, list as many good things in your life as you can. Thank God for each one of them.

BONE TIRED

Read Matthew 11:28-30.

Jesus said, "Come to me and I will give you rest."

Mark Ingram was tired. He just wanted to sit out a few plays. So all he did was put the Tide on his back and carry them to a win.

On Oct. 17, 2009, against South Carolina, the sophomore tailback had set a personal high of 178 yards rushing, and there was still a lot of time left in the fourth quarter.

That was the good news. The bad news was that he was all Alabama had. The offense had been pretty awful all day. So South Carolina trailed only 13-6 with about eight minutes left to play. "We were right there," said the Gamecocks' head coach, Steve Spurrier.

Alabama got the ball after a South Carolina punt, but Ingram was just bone tired. He said he thought about staying out he was so tired.

Crimson Tide

But the Tide coaches had no choice. He had to carry the ball no matter how tired he was. And he did: six straight times! The last carry went for a touchdown. Mark Ingram had taken Alabama 68 yards down the field by himself.

Behind its tired tailback, Bama won 20-6. And Mark Ingram was on his way to winning the 2009 Heisman Trophy.

Don't you just get tired sometime? Maybe after a tough day at school when you stayed up too late the night before. Have you ever gotten so tired on a trip that you fell asleep in the back seat of the car?

Everybody gets tired, especially grown-ups. And sometimes, like grown-ups, you have to do what Mark Ingram had to do. You have to finish something no matter how tired you are.

That's a good time to pray to Jesus. When you do that, you have the power of almighty God to help you and give you strength.

Talk about the last time you fell asleep on the floor. Why were you so tired? Did you know God can give you strength?

THE INTERVIEW

Read Romans 14:9-12.

We will all have to explain to God everything we have done.

One of Alabama's greatest coaches ever was never interviewed for the job.

When a grown-up wants a job at Alabama, he or she must have an interview. He answers questions from the people who will hire him so they will know something about him.

Sarah Patterson was the head coach of the Crimson Tide gymnastics team for 36 years. She retired in 2014 because of her health. Her teams won six national titles and eight SEC championships. She was a head coach at Alabama longer than anybody else.

Her teams had more than 1,000 wins. That's about 200 more than the Tide football team has had in its whole history!

Patterson was only 22 years old when Coach

Crimson Tide

Bear Bryant hired her in 1978. But the Bear named her head coach without an interview, which is really odd.

He first hired her as an assistant coach. Before she ever showed up to coach, she got a letter telling her that she wasn't the assistant coach anymore. She was now the head coach. Sarah Patterson was hired through the mail!

You've probably never had a job interview, but you will one day. You may have an interview to get into some school club or group.

Interviews are hard because people ask you questions and judge you. That means they decide whether you are good enough for what they want. Nobody likes to be judged.

One day, you will show up in Heaven. The Bible tells us that we all will be judged by God. We will have an interview with God.

Talk about being nervous! How in the world can we be good enough for God? All it takes is Jesus. Jesus makes us good enough.

Pretend you're being interviewed by God. What would you tell him about yourself?

TEAM PLAYERS

Read 1 Corinthians 12:4-6.

People have different gifts and different ways to serve. But they all come from the same God.

How did Bama go from a so-so 6-6 record in 2007 to a fantastic 12-0 in 2008? Nick Saban knew it was a team thing.

The Alabama head coach couldn't say exactly when things changed. "It's not something that's a one-time thing," he said.

What happened is that after the 6-6 season, the players figured out that what they were doing wasn't good enough. They didn't want to be 6-6 anymore. They were Alabama football players; they should be better than that. "We needed to make a change," said one player.

Alabama beat Colorado 30-24 in the 2007 PetroSun Independence Bowl. Then the whole team — not just a player or two — went to work.

Crimson Tide

All winter, they worked in the weight room. In the heat of the summer, every single player showed up for drills, even though they didn't have to.

The players also treated each other like teammates. They didn't see another player as just someone trying to beat them out for playing time.

As a real team, Alabama went undefeated during the regular season in 2008.

Have you ever thought that a church is just like a football team? In your church, the people share a faith with you. Like a team, they all work toward the same goal: growing stronger in their faith and teaching people about Jesus.

Of course, the people in your church are all different. Some are old, and some are young. Some men, some women. Some short, some tall. Some can sing, some can't.

They all have talents that they use for the team. Then the church becomes a winner.

You're on the church team. What talents can you bring to help the church win?

ANIMAL FARM

Read Genesis 6:13-21.

God told Noah to take two of every living thing into the ark.

Don McNeal could not kill Kate no matter how hard he tried.

Don grew up on a farm, chopping cotton and picking peas. His dad didn't have a tractor; he had Kate. She was a mule, a former rodeo star he had bought for $75.

When his older brothers grew up, Don got the job of plowing behind Kate. She never got tired, so Don decided to kill her before she worked him to death. He first tried to starve her. Then he tried giving her too much water, so she'd have a heat stroke. Nothing worked.

Then Don came up with a plan he was sure would work. One day, he loaded Kate into the back of the pickup truck. He sped off and raced around a curve. As Don put it, "The ol' gal flew out of the back of the truck" and bounced down a hill. He just knew Kate was dead. But when Don looked down that hill, there was Kate standing up and looking right at him.

Don McNeal escaped Kate and the farm by being an All-American cornerback at Alabama, playing on the 1978 and 1979 national champs. He played ten years in the pros.

We love our pets. Have you ever thought that God loves them, too? Your dog, your cat, even your fish — they praise God every day by being what God made them to be.

God showed how much he loved his animals when he told Noah to pack them into the ark. God saved all his varmints, not just some of the people. That tells you that all the creatures of this Earth are under God's care.

That also says you are not to be mean to animals. You treat them kindly. You take care of them the way God takes care of you.

What kinds of pets do you have? What are the things you do to take good care of them the way God wants you to?

HUMBLE PIE

Read Matthew 23:9-12.

Those of you who humble yourselves will be raised up.

As an Alabama fan, you learn to be humble when the Tide loses the Iron Bowl.

To be humble means you don't think you're better than anybody else. Thank goodness, Jesus wasn't talking about the Iron Bowl and college football. You know for sure that Bama is better than Auburn and everybody else.

Kenny Stabler won 28 games as the Tide quarterback from 1965 through 1967. He once said that rubbing Auburn's nose "in the [pig] trough is a God-given right" after a win in the Iron Bowl. When you win, he said, you dish it out because you live with Auburn folks the whole year. You remind Auburn fans of how good Alabama is for a year, not just a week.

That works the other way, too. One time,

Crimson Tide

Coach Bear Bryant was relaxing at his cabin on a lake. Suddenly, a whole bunch of boats rode by, and everyone in them screamed out, "War Eagle!" Even on his vacation, Coach Bryant couldn't get away from Auburn fans.

The only way to teach them some humility is to beat them in the next Iron Bowl.

Jesus told us Christians are to be humble. Sometimes it's hard, isn't it?

But Jesus doesn't mind that you pull for the Tide and think Alabama is Number One. When Jesus said you are to be humble, he meant you are to be a servant for others. That means you do nice things for other people. You help someone at school when she needs it. You don't act snooty toward other kids.

But here's something funny. One day, all those who love Jesus will be with him. Then, those who are humble in this life will be the ones whom God will say are the best.

Have you ever thought you were better than someone else? Why? Does God think you're better than someone else?

ORPHANS NO MORE

Read 1 John 3:1-3.

God loves us so much he calls us his children.

Once upon a time, so few folks went to Alabama basketball games that the team was known as "Alabama's Orphan Five."

Alabama played its first basketball game in 1913. The ceiling of the gym was so low that when a player tried a long shot, the ball hit the ceiling and bounced to the floor! Only a few people showed up for the games, leading the papers to refer to the players as orphans.

Nobody cared much about basketball. One time in 1916, a game was stopped before the time ran out. Why would they do that? So everyone could leave the game and get to a glee club concert on time!

The team didn't even have a full-time coach as it does now. One of the players acted as the coach.

So every year, the papers said the school wouldn't field a basketball team next season since nobody really cared. That ended in 1921 when the first full-time basketball coach was hired. The team was orphans no more.

An orphan is a child whose parents have died. Most people feel sorry for them because they sometimes don't have anybody to take care of them or to love them. Jesus loved them. In fact, he told us to take care of them.

Jesus gave us a whole lot of promises while he was on this Earth. One of his last was one of his greatest. He said that if we follow him, we will be God's children.

So if you have decided to follow Jesus, you are God's adopted child. You may not be an orphan, but you are still a child of God. That means God loves you. You are one of God's children forever. How cool is that!

Draw a picture of your parents. Include God in the picture since you are one of God's children because you love Jesus.

THE ALABAMA WAY

Read Romans 13:10-12.

Behave decently like in the daytime, the way Jesus would.

It looked like Bear Bryant was trying to make his quarterback feel better. But he wasn't. He was telling him about The Alabama Way.

From 1962 through 1964, Joe Namath was the Tide quarterback. He went 29-4 and led the team to the 1964 national title. Coach Bryant said Namath was "the greatest athlete I ever coached." In turn, Namath said the Bear "was the smartest coach I ever knew."

But Namath was from Pennsylvania, so he had a lot to learn about the way things were done in Tuscaloosa. He had to learn The Alabama Way, the way a Tide player acts both on and off the football field.

Against Vanderbilt in 1962, he learned some of that. Namath was playing badly. Mad at himself, he slammed his helmet to the ground as he headed to the bench. Coach Bryant came over, sat down, and put an arm around him. It looked like he was being nice to him.

He wasn't. "He was nearly squeezing my head off," Namath said. "Boy," the coach said. "Don't you ever let me see you throw your helmet around and act like a show-off." Acting like that wasn't The Alabama Way.

Even as a young person, you have a certain way that you live. You're an Alabama fan. Maybe you live in the country. Or in town. Do you wear jeans to school? Or shorts? You have a favorite video game and TV show.

Then there's your faith. Like Coach Bryant, you're a Christian. As a way of life, you follow Jesus. You do your best to act and to think like Jesus would. That means you always try to act in a loving manner toward other people.

It's The Jesus Way. It should be your way.

List some ways you can follow the Jesus way at school. Then remember them and try to do them.

KNOW-IT-ALLS

Read Matthew 13:10-12.

Jesus told his disciples, "I have let you know the secrets of the kingdom of heaven."

Billy Neighbors thought he was at Alabama just to play football and not to study. Coach Bear Bryant let him know he didn't know it all.

An All-American lineman in 1961, Neighbors played both ways; that means he played both offense and defense. He loved football, but he didn't care much about studying. He thought Coach Bryant didn't care that he was missing a lot of classes.

Then one day the coach asked Neighbors to eat lunch with him. He had a school dean with him. That's kind of like your school principal. He also had a record of every grade Neighbors had made and every class he had cut.

The coach surprised Neighbors by telling

him he had to move into his house. He told his lineman he was going to treat him just like he had done his son once. "When he comes home with a C, I'll beat him with a dictionary," the head coach said.

"I got straightened out real fast!" Neighbors said. As it turned out, he didn't know it all, but Coach Bryant sure did.

Do you like school? You might as well. In today's world, if you don't finish high school, you probably won't get a good job. You should want to go to college after high school. Maybe — if you study real hard — even Alabama!

You can study and learn a lot about history and science, for instance. But no matter how much you study, you can't learn all there is to know about God. Except for one thing. God has told you how to get to Heaven.

All you need to know about Jesus and the way to Heaven is right there in the Bible. You just need to read it and study it.

List some things you don't know about God, such as what he looks like.

HUGS AND KISSES

Read John 15:9-14.

Jesus said, "I have loved you. Now remain in my love."

Coaches have to work real hard to get high school athletes to come play for Alabama. But all it took for softball coach Patrick Murphy to land one of his greatest players was a hug.

Brittany Rogers was All-SEC and All-America all four seasons at Alabama. Murphy called her the fastest player he had ever had. She was so fast she set a school record for stealing bases. When she was a senior in 2009, she won the award as Alabama's best female athlete.

Two Crimson Tide assistant coaches first saw Brittany play when she was in high school. They noticed right off that she was a hugger. So they told Coach Murphy, "When you meet her, make sure you give her a hug."

Coach Murphy and Rogers swapped a lot of

e-mails before they finally met. He did what his coaches had told him; he hugged her. That did it! She decided to play her college ball for Alabama.

"I come from a very hugging family," the Alabama star explained. "Every time I see my mom or grandma or anyone, we always give each other a hug."

A hug is a sign of affection. When you hug someone, you're showing them you care for them. It doesn't just make them feel good; it makes you feel good, too. A hug is also a symbol. Holding someone close to you says how closely you hold them in your heart.

The greatest hugger of them all is God. Through Jesus, God tries to pull you closer to himbecause he loves you. A good hug takes two, so God wants you to hug him back.

You do that by loving Jesus. To love Jesus is to hug God — and that feels mighty good.

Do you like to hug people? Think of some folks you'd like to hug and then do it the next time you see them.

GOOD JOB

Read Matthew 25:14-21.

The boss said, "Good job, good and faithful worker."

Alabama once pulled off a goal-line stand so good that even Coach Bear Bryant took notice.

A goal line stand can happen only when the team with the ball is close to the other team's goal line. When the defense stops the team from scoring, that's a goal line stand.

A good goal-line stand lasts four plays. In 1981, against Penn State, Alabama had one that lasted seven plays. That's because the Tide drew a penalty in the middle of it.

How in the world could they do it? They were ready. Once a week, every week, they practiced for a goal-line stand. All-American safety Tommy Wilcox said for one hour each week, "You were constantly moving, people barfing into trash cans," running another play with the coaches screaming at you "when you didn't think you could take another step."

So on this day, it was "been there and done that" for Alabama when Penn State lined up and ran play after play. They ran seven plays inside the 10-yard line and didn't score.

When the defense reached the sideline, Coach Bryant took his hat off and tipped it at his players. He was telling his defense, "Good job, men."

Good job. Way to go. It's nice hearing those words, isn't it? Whether you've aced a test, helped out with a church play, or finished a science project. When you work hard, you like to have people notice and tell you.

The most important "good job" of all is the one that comes from God. As a Christian, you will meet God in Heaven one day. You will want God to say to you, "Well done. Good job."

Nothing else in life is as important as doing a good job for God.

Name some ways that you do a good job for God.

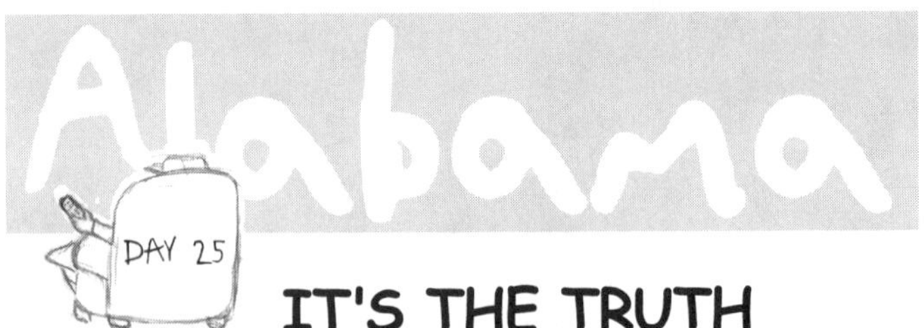

IT'S THE TRUTH

Read Matthew 5:33-37.

Jesus said, "If you mean 'yes,' say 'yes.' If you mean 'no,' say 'no.'"

His momma spoke the cold, hard truth, and Alabama kept one of its greatest quarterbacks.

Richard Todd started for three seasons (1973-75) at Alabama. The teams he led went 33-3; they won three SEC titles and the 1973 national championship. Alabama never lost an SEC game that Richard Todd started!

In high school, Todd didn't like the wishbone offense Alabama ran. He liked to throw the ball; the wishbone ran the ball a lot. Still, he decided to go to Alabama because Coach Bear Bryant "was the best coach in the country."

As a freshman in 1972, though, Todd was unhappy in Tuscaloosa. After a loss, he was really down. He hated the wishbone and was thinking about transferring to another school, one that didn't run the wishbone.

So he called his momma. He whined to her a little bit, expecting her to support him. Instead, she laid the hard truth on him. She said, "The way you played today, you wouldn't have helped anyone else, either."

She wouldn't let him blame everyone else for the loss. That bit of truth helped change his attitude. Next season Todd was the starter and was on his way to greatness.

Unlike Richard Todd's momma, sometimes we lie to avoid hurting someone else's feelings. Or to make ourselves look better. Or to get out of trouble.

But Jesus says you are always to tell the truth. As far as Jesus is concerned, telling the truth is right; lying is wrong.

Lying is what the devil ("the evil one") does. God cannot lie; the devil lies as a way of life. Whose side are you on when you tell a lie?

Recall a lie you told to get out of trouble. Did it make you feel good? Do you think God was proud of you for lying?

CONTROL FREAK

Read Matthew 19:16-22.

The young man went away sad because he wasn't willing to give away his money to follow Jesus.

Coach Dave Rader wanted to get control of a play so badly that he did something kind of really dumb.

Coach Rader was the offensive coordinator for Alabama in 2005. He was way up in the press box above Bryant-Denny Stadium during the 2005 game against Arkansas. From up there, he could see the whole field and help the head coach call the plays for the offense.

Alabama led only 17-13 in the fourth quarter when Rader called a run right up the middle. But when the Tide lined up, Rader went berserk. He started pounding on the window of the press box. Why? He was trying to get the attention of quarterback Brodie Croyle. There he was, at the top of the stadium, banging on the glass. "How stupid is that?" Rader asked. "Like Brodie's going to hear me."

He saw a wide open play, a sure touchdown. Croyle saw it, too, even though he couldn't hear the coach. He changed the play and threw a touchdown pass to clinch the 24-13 win.

At your age, you don't have control of much. People tell you what time to go to bed, what TV shows to watch, where to sit in the car. As a kid, you can't control what other people do.

Here's a secret: Grown-ups can't either, not really. For instance, they can't control whether or not another person loves Jesus. That means they have no control of whether someone else is saved and is going to Heaven. Even Jesus left it up to the rich young man to decide if he would make the Son of God his lord.

Like grown-ups, all you can do is tell people about Jesus. After that, it's up to them. You can't control them and how they respond.

Name some things you can control. Loving Jesus should be on that list.

GOOD-BYE

Read John 13:33-36.

Jesus told Peter, "Where I am going, you can't follow now."

On the day Gene Stallings said good-bye, his team gave him a perfect going-away gift.

On Jan. 1, 1997, the Tide whipped Michigan 17-14 in the Outback Bowl. Stallings had previously announced his retirement as Alabama's head football coach; this was his last game.

Stallings loved defense, and in the Outback Bowl, his defense carried the day. Michigan led early 6-3 and was on its way to scoring again, but the Bama defense rose up. Linebacker Dwayne Rudd stepped in front of a pass for an interception. He had a convoy of blockers in front of him and went 88 yards for a touchdown. "I saw some green and I ran to it," Rudd said.

The Tide never trailed again. Alabama led 17-6 before Michigan managed a late touchdown that did nothing but change the score.

Stallings left the field for the last time on the shoulders of his players. They had told their coach good-bye with the kind of game he loved: a defensive battle.

Even though you're a youngster, you have probably known good-byes — and they hurt. Maybe your best friend moved away. Maybe you moved away and had to tell a whole lot of your friends and buddies good-bye. It's sad to stand and wave while your grandparents drive off on their way home after a visit.

Jesus knows just how you feel. He always had his friends around him, but it came time for him to tell them good-bye. He was going away; he would leave them.

But Jesus wasn't just moving to another town. He was about to finish his mission on Earth. He would provide a way so that none of us would ever have to say good-bye again.

List some people you have said good-bye to. Get their addresses from a parent and write them a note.

NOT WHAT THEY SEEM

Read Habakkuk 1:2-4.

God, why do you put up with all the bad stuff people do?

You would think moving to the pros from the college game would be a step up. Not always.

Sports Illustrated called former Tide guard John Hannah "the best offensive lineman of all time" when he was in the NFL. He was a star on the Alabama teams of 1971 and 1972 that went 21-3 and won two SEC titles. An All-America, he was drafted by the New England Patriots.

Hannah had a great pro career, going to the Pro Bowl ten times. He was the first Patriot to make it into the Pro Football Hall of Fame.

So all that glitz of pro football must have been special for Hannah, right? Well, no. He said the pros were actually a step down from Alabama.

His first year a writer asked him what it felt

Crimson Tide

like to play in front of 55,000 people. Hannah said it would be disappointing. The guy looked at him like he was nuts. Hannah said, "You've got to remember, I've been playing in front of 80,000 people for the last three years."

The pros seemed big-time, but it was Alabama that was the real big-time.

You know, sometimes things just aren't what they seem. It's like a mirror in a fun house at the fair. Have you ever seen one of those? It makes you look all wacky and distorted.

It's that way with the world; it looks like nobody's in charge. We have wars everywhere. People hurt and kill other people. Children go to bed hungry at night. What's going on?

That's what Habakkuk asked God long ago, and God answered him. God said things aren't what they seem. He said he was in control and one day he would make everything all right.

You just have to trust and believe in God.

As Habakkuk did, name some things you'd like to see God change about this world. Pray for those changes.

THE WINNER'S CIRCLE

Read 1 John 5:1-6.

The person who believes Jesus is the son of God is the real winner in the world.

It's hard to believe, but there was a time when Alabama wasn't winning on the football field. That all changed on Dec. 3, 1957.

From 1955 through 1957, the Tide won only four games. As one person put it, "The bottom line was that things were bad."

After a dismal 1957 season, school bigwigs hired a new coach. He was Paul "Bear" Bryant. "I came here to make Alabama a winner again," he told his players. And he did.

He said the first thing he had to find out was how many of his players were winners. At the first practice, they saw the walls of the gym lined with garbage pails for vomiting.

The winning began with Coach Bryant's first

Crimson Tide

first season and never stopped. Someone said, "No college football coach built winning football teams better than Bryant."

From 1958 through 1982, the Tide won six national championships and thirteen SEC titles. When the first practice began in 1958, Alabama was on its way to glory – and winning.

Life is a competition; it's not just football or soccer games. You compete against others at school for a good seat in the lunchroom. You try to beat others in a video game.

Competition isn't bad for you as long as you play according to the rules the way that Coach Bryant's teams did. It makes you stronger.

In everything you do, you should want to win. Winning isn't everything, but you should always try to do your best. Sometimes you will lose, but you don't quit trying.

Only with your faith in Jesus do you never lose. You win — for all time.

Name some things in which you competed and won and some you lost. Did they make you feel different? How?

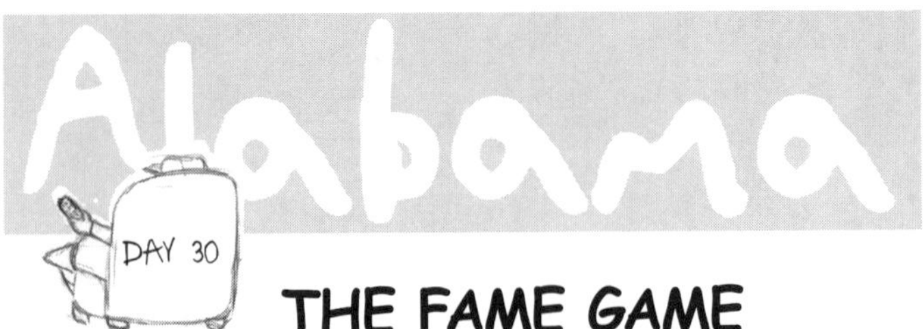

THE FAME GAME

Read 1 Kings 10:23-25.

Solomon was so famous people all over the world wanted to meet him.

Girls screamed his name. Folks nearly broke down a fence to get his autograph. Not bad for a player a lot of people thought was dead.

Brodie Croyle ranks among Alabama's best quarterbacks ever. As a senior in 2005, he set a record by passing for 2,499 yards. He led the Crimson Tide to a 10-2 season and a win in the Cotton Bowl.

Before the season started, a rumor ran around that Brodie had been killed hunting in Argentina. (Look it up on a globe.) One story said his dad and he had been killed in a car wreck. Another story said he had died after being kidnapped. None of this was true, and that was a good thing for Alabama fans.

The best game of Brodie's career was on

Crimson Tide

Oct. 8 against No. 5 Florida. Alabama routed the favored Gators 31-3 behind Brodie's great game that included three touchdown passes.

In the last minutes of the game, Alabama fans swooped down on the fence behind the Tide bench. They screamed out, "Bro-deee!" Someone said it was just like the famous rock group the Beatles had come to town.

A lot of grown-ups want to be famous like the people on TV or in the movies. Fame just means that complete strangers know your name or face. Alabama football players are like that. A lot people whom they've never met know their names and what they look like.

Are you famous? The answer may surprise you. That's because you are famous where it really counts. Alabama's football players may not know you, but God does.

God knows your name, what you look like, and what size shoe you wear. You are famous in Heaven where God and the angels live.

Make a list of some people you think are famous. Was Jesus on the list?

EXCUSES, EXCUSES

Read Luke 9:59-62.

If you start to follow Jesus and then make excuses not to serve him, you are not fit for Heaven.

While everybody else was making excuses, the Tide went out and won the tournament.

SEC basketball coaches were very unhappy when the 1982 conference basketball tournament was played on Kentucky's home court. After Ole Miss lost to Kentucky, the Rebel head coach said his team lost because of a "home-cooked rat." He meant the referees called the game Kentucky's way.

So amid all the coaches' whining and complaining, Alabama went out and upset Kentucky in the finals. In a smart move, Bama coach Wimp Sanderson figured he couldn't do anything about the big Kentucky home crowd. So he quieted them by slowing the game down.

Crimson Tide

With the score tied at 46 and time running out, Alabama put up an air ball. But senior Eddie Phillips grabbed the ball and flipped it up and in the basket just as the game ended.

Alabama made no excuses. They just won the game and went to the NCAA Tournament.

You've made some excuses before, haven't you? What excuse did you use when you didn't do your homework? Have you ever said you felt bad so you didn't have to do something?

Lots of folks make excuses when we don't like the way things are going. Or when stuff gets too hard. Or we fail at something.

We do it with our faith life, too. We say the Bible's too hard to read. The weather's too pretty to be shut up in church. Or praying in public is downright embarrassing.

But, you know, Jesus died for you without making any excuses. The least you can do is live for him with no excuses.

What excuse did you use the last time you didn't say your prayers at bedtime? Did you think God liked that excuse?

TEST CASE

Read James 1:2-6, 12.

The person is blessed who keeps on going when times are hard.

Almost every day at school, you have a test of some sort. Alabama head coach Frank Thomas knew exactly how you feel.

After his resignation in 1930 as Bama's head football coach, Wallace Wade recommended Thomas for the job. He told school president George H. Denny (who, with Bear Bryant has the stadium named after him), "I don't believe you could pick a better man."

Dr. Denny was the first Alabama president to decide that the school would be a football power. He met with Thomas and said, "Material is 90 percent, coaching ability 10 percent." He told Thomas he as the school president would provide the 90 percent; the coach had to deliver the other ten percent. He would be fired if he didn't.

A surprised Thomas asked a newsman if he thought Denny's figures were right. The man said he didn't know, but there was no doubt that the good doctor meant what he said.

So, Thomas' entire career at Alabama was one long test. He aced it. He won 115 games and two national championships.

Tests stress us all out because they tell us how well we are doing something. We worry about them because we all fear failing.

But you know something? It's not the tests in life that use a paper and pen that are the hardest to pass. It's the times that you face trouble and disappointment and want to quit.

Like Coach Thomas' career at Bama with Dr. Denny watching him every day, life is one long test. You need to remember that. Remember, too, that God wants you to pass. He even gave you the answer to life's tests: Jesus.

Make up a test with questions on it that God might ask you. Give your answers and decide whether you'd pass.

CELEBRATION TIME

Read Luke 15:8-10.

Heaven celebrates every time a sinner turns away from his sin.

Steadman Shealy celebrated only one time in his Alabama career. It was when he pulled off what one writer called one of the greatest plays in Tide football history.

Shealy quarterbacked the Tide during the last three seasons of the 1970s. The team was a sensational 34-2 with him as the leader. The Tide won three SEC titles and two national championships.

Alabama was ranked No. 1 for the Iron Bowl in 1979, but Auburn was good, too. The Tigers led 18-17 with about eight minutes to play.

Alabama put together a drive to try and pull the game out. With the ball at the Auburn 8, Shealy held the ball on the wishbone and raced around the end for a touchdown.

Crimson Tide

That's when he celebrated for the only time. And what did he do? "I jumped up and patted the ball," he said. "The other guys came over and celebrated too." Alabama won 25-18.

A book published years later listed Shealy's touchdown as Alabama's 13th greatest play.

Have you ever whooped and hollered when Alabama scored a touchdown? Or maybe you just smiled and felt good inside the first time you got a hit in a softball or baseball game.

When we're happy about something that just happened or something we did, we celebrate. We also celebrate special days, like your birthday or Easter Sunday.

Did you know God and the angels celebrate, too? They sing and shout and throw a party quite often. They celebrate every time someone accepts Jesus as their savior.

Just think. When you said "yes" to Jesus, you made the angels dance.

What did you do to celebrate your last birthday? Why does your family celebrate Christmas?

THINGS HAPPEN

Read Isaiah 55:8-11.

God's thoughts are not like ours, and God's ways are different from ours.

Alabama wound up with one of its greatest players ever because of a flat tire.

From 1972 through 1975, Woodrow Lowe was such a great linebacker that he wound up in the Hall of Fame. He and Cornelius Bennett are the Tide's only three-time All-Americas.

Until something happened that looked like it was a bad break, Lowe was headed to Auburn to play football.

A high-school teammate and he had been invited by the Tigers to come watch a game. As Lowe put it, his friend had a beat-up old car. They had a flat tire on their way to the game and didn't have a spare. So they had to hitchhike to Auburn.

Crimson Tide

The game was over by the game they got there. They didn't see any Auburn coaches, who probably figured Lowe wasn't interested in playing for them. They never got in touch with him again. And yet, Lowe said, if they had just called him back, he probably would have gone there.

Fortunately for Alabama, it was just one of those things that happen sometimes.

Things happen to you, too, don't they? Maybe when it started raining just as you were all set to go swimming. Or the time you got real sick, and the doctor had to give you a shot.

You don't know why stuff like that happens. The truth is God doesn't tell us why. His ways are different from ours. After all, he is God and we are not. So we don't know what's going to happen next. It catches us by surprise.

God just asks that you trust him. He is the one in charge, and everything will be all right for those who trust in Jesus.

List three things that happened to you that you really don't know why they did.

MIRACLE PLAY

Read Matthew 12:38-40.

Jesus said, "Wicked and unfaithful people ask for miracles" to convince them he is Lord and Savior.

Coach Bear Bryant could work miracles with his football teams. But could he really control the weather?

Alabama went 11-0 in 1966, but the Tide was a big underdog to Nebraska in the 1967 Sugar Bowl. The weather didn't help Alabama either. It rained all weekend long before the game and was raining while the teams warmed up. A wet field helped Nebraska since they ran the ball better than Alabama did.

Everybody said the Tide needed a miracle. They got one. Bama quarterback Ken Stabler remembered what happened just as the team came out of the locker room to start the game. "When Coach Bryant stepped onto the field it quit raining! It did!" he said.

Then right before the kickoff, Bryant walked up to Stabler and told him to throw the ball as far as he could on the first play. Stabler did. He hit Ray Perkins, who coached Bama from 1983 through 1986, for a 45-yard gain. A few plays later, the Tide scored.

The game was over. With a help from the Bear's weather miracle, Alabama won 34-7.

A miracle is something that you can't explain except by saying God did it. Some people say miracles are rare, but they are wrong.

Since God made the world and everything in it, the whole world is a miracle. You are a miracle! Just think: There's nobody else in the world like you. You're so special God made only one of you (unless you're a twin!).

A lot of people don't see miracles around them because they don't have any faith in God. Jesus knew that seeing a miracle doesn't make someone believe in him. But you believe in Jesus and God, so you do see miracles.

List some things around you that are miracles because God made them.

YOU PROMISED

Read 2 Peter 1:3-7.

God's promises are great and valuable.

One time an Alabama player kept a promise to an injured teammate. The result was an SEC championship.

Alabama went 16-2 in the 1934 basketball season, losing twice to Kentucky. Right before the tournament, though, Zeke Kimbrough, the leading scorer, was injured in practice. He had surgery and was in the hospital.

The team visited Kimbrough in the hospital. His best friend, Jimmy Walker, made his buddy and teammate a promise. "We are going to win it for you," he told Kimbrough. "That's a promise and I don't break promises."

Kimbrough made it to the tournament. The school president arranged for him to sit on the bench. He had his picture made with his teammates.

And they made good on the promise Jimmy Walker had made. The Tide beat Miss. State, edged Tennessee by three points, and blew past Florida 41-25 for the title. Walker was the leading scorer in the win over the Gators.

Alabama was the SEC champion. Promise made and promise kept.

You should never make any promises lightly. That means that if you promise somebody something, you should keep it, even if it costs you or is a lot of trouble.

Sometimes your friends and even grown-ups don't keep their promises. But God doesn't work that way. If God makes a promise, he keeps it, and in the Bible, God makes thousands of promises! Peter calls them "great and valuable" because God makes them and then keeps them.

You can count on God to keep his promises.

Recall the last promise you made. Whom did you make it to? Did you keep it? If you didn't keep it, why not?

BEING ALIKE

Read Philippians 3:8-11.

I want to be like Jesus.

Rolando McClain and Nick Saban apparently shared a brain.

McClain was a first-team All-America and the SEC Defensive Player of the Year for the 2009 national champions. His teammates were the ones who noticed that McClain and his head coach thought a lot alike. Saban agreed. "I'm a perfectionist, and I think he's a perfectionist," he said about his star. "He likes to get things right."

When a player was injured in the Arkansas game, the coaches had to move several of the players around. McClain took over like his head coach on the field. He made sure each player knew what he was supposed to do in his new position. Alabama won 35-7.

McClain was so much like Saban he could

even know what the coach would want to do sometimes. In the SEC championship game, Alabama beat Florida 32-13. As the clock ticked down, some players got ready to dump Gatorade on Saban. McClain stopped them.

"It wasn't the right time," he said. He knew that Saban wouldn't want Gatorade poured on him until Alabama won the national title.

Have you ever been told you look like somebody else? Maybe your mom or your dad? Most kids do look like a family member.

More important than that, though, is who you act like. Some grown-ups want to look like and act like movie stars or football players. There is really only one person worth acting like. It is Jesus.

We can never be exactly like Jesus. Each day, however, we can try to be a little more like Jesus than we were the day before. To be a Christian means you spend your life becoming more like Jesus.

Name some ways you acted like Jesus today. Name some ways you didn't.

YOUR GOAL

Read 1 Peter 1:7-9.

Because of your faith, you are receiving your goal, which is the salvation of your soul.

Stephen Bolt had a clear goal even when coaches changed the rules to make it hard for him.

Four-zero-zero." That was Bolt's goal. He had the numbers all over his apartment. They stood for four minutes and zero seconds. In 1976, Bolt ran the mile on Alabama's track team, and he was one of the best ever. His goal was to run a mile in under four minutes.

Right before the SEC championships, he ran a mile in 3:58 in practice. "I knew I was ready to break the four-minute mark," he said. He was ready to reach his goal.

But he was so good that the SEC coaches voted to put in an extra race before the finals.

Crimson Tide

Everyone called it the "Steve Bolt Rule." "They were trying to wear me down," Bolt said.

It looked like his goal was out of reach. He might win the mile run in the finals, but he would be too tired to run the mile in under four minutes.

Bolt simply ran as fast as he could. He first won the two-mile race and then ran the mile race in 3:59:4. He had reached his goal.

You have goals in your life. Maybe to get better at soccer, math, or a video game. Or to make all A's in school. Maybe you want to earn a spot in the band or on the track team.

You have goals in your faith life, too. You go to church to worship God. You read the Bible to learn more about God. But what's your goal? What is all that stuff about?

The goal of your faith life is to get to Heaven. If you are saved by believing in Jesus, then someday you will be with Jesus and with God in Heaven.

Make a list of the goals you want to reach in school and in church this year.

SWEET WORDS

Read Romans 8:35-39.

Nothing can separate you from God's love because of what Jesus Christ has done.

John David Phillips wasn't sure he had done the right thing until God sent him a message.

In 1995, Phillips was moved to wide receiver for the Alabama football team. It was a good move; he was doing well. But Phillips couldn't sleep at night because he wasn't at peace with the move. He prayed about it until he came to believe that he should be playing quarterback.

He went to see head coach Gene Stallings and said he believed God wanted him to play quarterback. The head coach said he wasn't going to argue with God.

As Phillips walked toward his car, he prayed that God would send him a message that told him he had done the right thing. Before he got to his car, he met Tony Johnson, a tight end and a devout Christian. Johnson told Phillips, "You may find this odd. I feel like God wants you to play quarterback." Johnson said he had been praying and reading his Bible the night before when God had spoken to him.

Phillips now knew that his decision was one God had wanted him to make.

John David Phillips received what is called "affirmation." It's when you say something to someone that is good for them. You tell someone their clothes look nice, or you high-five a teammate and tell him, "Way to go."

Most of all, you affirm someone when you tell them that God loves them. Nobody is better at affirmation than Jesus. He tells us that we mean a lot to God, that God loves us so much he died for us on a cross.

Because of that, nothing can ever separate you from God. Those are the sweetest words of all!

Think of some ways you can affirm somebody tomorrow at school and do it.

LESSON LEARNED

Read Psalm 143:8-11.

Teach me what you want me to do because you are my God.

Bear Bryant once learned a lesson from eating in a restaurant.

In 1958, the Bear was on a recruiting trip and went into a restaurant for lunch. "Seems I'm the only white fella in the place," he said.

"A big ole man in tee shirt and cap" told the coach he probably wouldn't like the food there. On the menu that day was chitlins. "I bet you don't even know what chitlins are," he said. (They're pig intestines.) Bryant said he had probably eaten a mile of them in his life. As the Bear ate lunch, he talked with the owner, telling him he was the new coach at Alabama.

As Bryant left, the man asked the coach if he had a photo he could hang on the wall of his restaurant. He didn't, but he wrote the man's name and address on a napkin and promised to send him one. He did.

Years later, a lineman told Bryant he was going to Auburn. Then he called the coach back and said he was coming to Alabama. When Bryant asked him why he changed his mind, he said it was his grandpa. He still had that picture of the Bear hanging in his restaurant.

Bryant learned again the lesson that it didn't cost anything to be nice to people.

You learn lessons every day at school. Math, science, language arts. But life outside of your school teaches you lessons, too. How to bait a hook. How to dance. Good manners. In every case, somebody teaches you.

And you learn lessons about your faith, too. God set down in his book all you need to know about living a godly life. He even sent Jesus to show you how you are to treat other people.

Just like in the classroom, you need to be a good student to learn God's lessons.

What's your favorite subject?
What about it do you like the most?

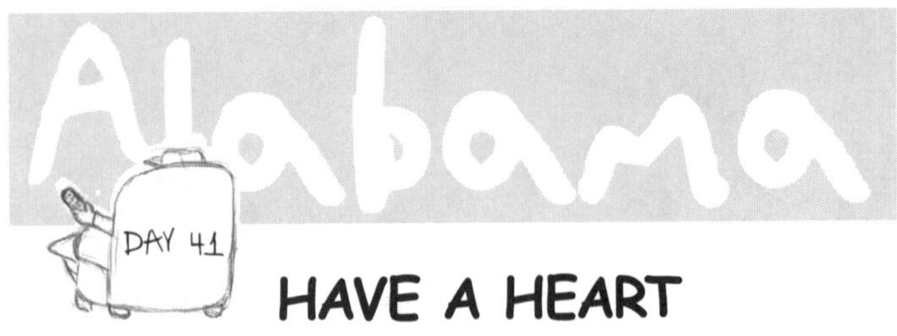

HAVE A HEART

Matthew 6:19-24.

You can't serve two masters. You will love one and hate the other.

Jim Wells retired twice as Alabama's baseball coach because he had a change of heart.

Wells won 625 games, more than any other Tide baseball coach. His teams won two SEC titles and six SEC tournaments.

In June 2007, Wells suddenly resigned. His boss, the athletic director, tried to get him to stay on the job, but Wells said he was determined to retire.

That retirement lasted only six days. That's when the coach went back to see the AD and told him he had had a change of heart. He wanted to stay on as baseball coach. The athletic director wasn't surprised at all. He hadn't even started looking for a new coach.

Plain and simple, Wells realized he had made

a mistake. "I haven't slept in six days," he said. "I saw how much I missed it." Wells' heart led him to change his mind about quitting. Only when he let it go did he see what he had and how much it meant to him.

So Wells retired in 2007 and then unretired. In 2009, he left for good. This time he knew in his heart it was the right thing to do.

Sometimes you must make a choice. Some other boys or girls might want you to do something that you know in your heart isn't right. Like cheat on a test or lie to your parents.

Your head says be cool and go along with the crowd. Your heart says it's wrong. How do you decide? Flip a coin? Use a dart board?

Nah. You turn to the one who should be number one in your life: Jesus. You figure out what Jesus would do.

Your head tells you what Jesus wants you to do. Your heart tells you that it is right to do it.

Pretend somebody wants to give you an answer to a test question. Make up an answer Jesus would give you about it.

MOMMA SAID

Read John 19:25-27.

Jesus' mother. Mary, stood near his cross.

Dwight Stephenson wasn't sure he was going to Alabama until his momma laid down the law.

Dwight's mom and dad worked had to provide a good life for their seven children in Virginia. His dad worked in the shipyards; his mom worked in the school cafeteria.

Dwight decided he would play college ball for Alabama. But then he started thinking about how far from home Tuscaloosa was. When two Tide coaches showed up for him to sign the scholarship, Dwight said he wasn't ready. Rather, he had decided to go to North Carolina State and play with two of his buddies.

When he told his momma that he wasn't going to Alabama, she wound that idea up in a hurry. "You're going to the University of Alabama," she said. That ended the discussion. Dwight went into the living room where the coaches were and signed with the Tide.

He was the starting center for three years at Alabama. He was All-America in 1979 and won the award as the SEC's best blocker. He is in the NFL Hall of Fame.

All because his momma put her foot down.

Mommas do a lot for their kids, and they do it all out of love. Even when your momma tells you to do something you don't want to, she has a good reason. It's usually for your good.

Think about Jesus' momma for a minute. She loved her boy no matter what. When Mary stood near the cross, she was showing both love and courage. No matter how wrong it was, Jesus was condemned as an enemy of the Roman Empire. She could have been, too.

Love your momma like she loves you.

Make a list of the things your momma did for you today. Did you thank her? Do you thank God for her?

FIRE IN YOUR HEART

Read Romans 12:9-16.

Never let the fire in your heart that burns for Jesus go out.

"I'm just too full of Alabama." So said Tommy Lewis, who loved Alabama so much that he pulled off one of the most famous — and most illegal — plays in college football history.

Lewis played fullback for Alabama for three seasons. He scored two touchdowns in the 61-6 defeat of Syracuse in the 1953 Orange Bowl. He is perhaps most famous for a play he made in the 1954 Cotton Bowl against Rice.

Rice's star running back was headed for a long touchdown run. Lewis suddenly flattened him. The crowd went silent except for a Rice cheerleader who screamed. "He did it!"

Lewis' tackle was a good clean hit. The only problem was that he wasn't in the game at the time. He was on the sideline when he stepped on the field and made the tackle.

The refs gave Rice the touchdown. After the game, Lewis went to the Rice locker room and apologized to the runner he had tackled. "I don't know what got into me," he said.

Tommy Lewis just couldn't help himself.

What makes you act the way Tommy Lewis did, like you have a fire in your heart?

It's probably not church, is it? Maybe you mumble the words to the songs while looking around at the ceiling. Or you sit there and look like you're in the waiting room at the dentist's office.

But God calls you to love him like you've got a fire in your heart or ants in your pants. You worship God because you love him. You love God because you can't help yourself.

Worshiping God is not some awful chore you have to endure. It should be one of the most joyous and exciting things you do.

Draw a picture of you with ants in your pants. Do you get that excited about going to church?

DANCING MACHINE

Read 2 Samuel 6:12-15.

In God's sight, David danced with joy as hard as he could.

The win was so big that even Tide head coach Nick Saban danced in celebration.

On Nov. 29, 2008, Alabama crushed Auburn 36-0 in the Iron Bowl. After the game, Tide players celebrated on the field. Some raised their helmets; others waved the school flag. Saban ran a victory lap before heading into the locker room.

So why all the celebration? It's not like the Tide hadn't beaten Auburn before.

Well, they hadn't for a while. Auburn had won six straight games in the series. Safety Rashad Johnson said beating Auburn was the goal for every one of the nine seniors. "We spent six years in a hole," he said.

Saban said the seniors would always be remembered for buying into what it took to play winning football at Alabama again.

And, yes, rumor has it that Saban did some celebrating in the locker room after the win. He led the team in the fight song and followed that up with a little victory jig.

Over the years, a lot of folks have believed Christians were always trying to make sure no one was having any fun.

But that is so wrong. Long ago, King David danced like crazy to honor God. And remember that Jesus was kin to David.

The truth is that if you love Jesus, you are saved. That's really something to be happy about. You should spend your life celebrating all the good things God has given you, especially Jesus.

Some people turn dancing and singing into something dirty. But God looks into your heart and knows what's there. You should be singing and dancing for Jesus.

Do you like singing and dancing? Make up a little dance in praise of God.

I TOLD YOU SO

Read Matthew 24:30-35.

Jesus will come on the clouds in power and glory.

Alabama basketball coach Mark Gottfried looked right at his team and told them they were going to win the game. They might not have believed him.

In the 2004 men's NCAA Tournament, the Tide played Stanford in the second round. The California team was a big favorite.

And they played like it. With only 7:42 left in the game, Stanford led by thirteen points and was pulling away. That's when Gottfried told his team they were going to win the game.

Somebody must have believed him. After the head coach's strange statement, Alabama scored sixteen straight points!

Stanford never did get over the shock. They tried fouling as the clock ran down; it didn't work. Alabama hit 12 of 16 free throws in the last 1:33 of the game.

The Tide won 70-67 to move on to the Sweet Sixteen for the first time since 1991. It all started when Coach Gottfried told them so.

One day Jesus is going to come back and find everyone who has been faithful to him. He will gather them all up and take them to Heaven. There they will live with God forever in happiness and love. It will be the most glorious time ever.

How do we know that's going to happen? Jesus told us so. When will it happen? Well, he didn't tell us that. He just told us to be ready so we don't miss it.

How do you get ready? It's simple. You just love Jesus. You live your life for Jesus. You remember that Jesus is counting on you, and you do everything for him.

Are you ready?

Put some ice cream in a bowl and watch it melt to remind you that Jesus may come back at any time, maybe even before the ice cream melts.

BELIEVE IT

Read John 3:16-18.

Whoever believes in Jesus will have eternal life.

Can you believe this? The Alabama players didn't want to play in the first SEC championship football game.

The SEC championship game is one of the biggest sports events of the year. Everybody wants tickets. The TV audience is really big.

The first game was played in 1992. No. 2 Alabama played No. 12 Florida. And the Tide players complained about having to play.

That's because they said they were playing for a championship they had already won with their perfect 12-0 season. End John Crawford said that if it weren't for this "newfangled title game," the players "could be sitting around playing cards." They could also have been getting ready to play (No. 1) Miami in the Sugar

Bowl for the national title. "All I know is, we've got practice this week," complained linebacker Michael Rogers.

Even if they didn't want to play, they did. And they won 28-21. Believe this: Alabama was the SEC champ and went on to win the national championship.

You believe a whole bunch of things without thinking about them. That the sun will come up tomorrow. That you will have a bed to sleep in tonight. That your parents love you. And you believe Jesus is the Son of God.

But not everybody in the world believes that part about Jesus. In fact, a lot of people, maybe even some in your school, will try to talk you out of believing in Jesus.

But they are really, really wrong. You just go right ahead and tell them about Jesus like he told you to. And then, say a prayer for them that they will come to believe.

Make a list of some things you believe. What if you didn't believe them? How would your life be different?

BE PREPARED

Read Matthew 10:5-10, 16.

Go into the world and be as wise as snakes and as innocent as doves.

An Alabama coach did something strange one time to get his team ready for a game. He had them watch a team Alabama wasn't going to play.

It sounds funny now but nobody thought Alabama football was very good way back in 1922. So Coach Xen Scott scheduled a game against Pennsylvania, which was a really good team back then. Nobody gave Bama a chance.

Coach Scott was called "a thinker, one of the brainiest coaches in the South." He came up with a way to help his team get ready.

They rode on the train, not to Pennsylvania, but to Washington, D.C. There the Tide players watched Navy play Penn State. Alabama came away from the game believing they could play with all those big teams from the East.

They did just that. They played Penn in front of the largest crowd ever to watch an Alabama game and they won 9-7.

Because Coach Scott did something kind of funny to prepare his team, everybody realized Southern football was pretty good.

Anytime Bama plays any game, the coaches and the players spend time preparing so they can win. It's the same way for you, isn't it?

When you have a test at school, you prepare by studying. You prepare for a ball game, a play, or a 4-H competition by practicing for it.

Jesus prepared his followers, too. He knew that he was going to die on the cross. He wanted them to be ready to spread the good news even after he went to Heaven.

You read the Bible and go to Sunday school and church. It's all to prepare you, so that one day you, too, will be ready to meet Jesus.

List the things you do in the morning to prepare for each day (like brush your teeth). Is a prayer on that list?

SOUND OFF!

Read Revelation 5:11-13.

I heard thousands and thousands of angels singing.

Alabama once had a player who made faces and shouted at the other team during a basketball game.

Billy Crews played on the 1954 Alabama team that went 16-8. He had a slightly different approach to the game. He figured that anything he could do to get a player's mind off the game would help him and the Tide.

So before a game started, Crews practiced making funny faces. He also took out his false front tooth to make his face look even funnier. Then when he got on the court during a game, he made faces at the other players. And he hollered at them as loud as he could.

Needless to say, Alabama fans loved Crews' shenanigans. Opposing players hated them.

Crimson Tide

One newspaper said Crews looked like Lon Chaney on the court. Chaney was a star who made monster movies. The paper said that away from a basketball game, Crews looked just like any other student. On the court, however, he was "a sight." And a sound.

You may not have shouted at players from another team, but you're used to a lot of noise, aren't you? Your school is noisy; football, basketball, and soccer games are noisy. Car horns blow, dogs bark, televisions shout.

You live in a noisy world. It's fun, but if you let it, all that noise will drown out the gentle voice of God in your heart. That means you need some quiet time every day. You can say your prayers, talk to God, and then listen for what he may have to say to you.

Much about Heaven will be strange, but one thing will make you feel right at home. As the Bible says, it's a noisy place. That's because everybody's whooping it up for God.

Get a watch to time yourself. Stay quiet and think about God for three minutes.

DEAD WRONG

Read Matthew 26:14-16; 27:1-5.

Judas was ashamed and sad because he had betrayed Jesus.

Mark Ingram proved a lot of people wrong when he won the Heisman Trophy. That included the greatest coach of all, Bear Bryant.

It took 74 years for a Tide football player to win college football's biggest individual prize. Bama was the only top football program in the country that had never had a Heisman winner.

Ingram didn't look like the one who would break the streak. The experts said that in high school he was a good player but not a great one. So a lot of programs didn't recruit him.

Alabama did and, boy, were they glad! In 2009, Ingram, a running back, was the best player on the Crimson Tide team. And Alabama won the national championship.

When the season ended, Ingram won the

Crimson Tide

Heisman Trophy as the best college football player in the whole country.

He proved all those recruiters wrong. He also proved Coach Bryant wrong. The Bear once said that Crimson Tide players didn't win Heisman trophies. They won national titles instead. Mark Ingram did both.

Everybody's wrong at some time or other. Maybe you walked into the wrong classroom at school. How many times have you come up with the wrong answer on a test?

Here's a secret: Even grown-ups are wrong.

Think about Judas. He turned Jesus over to folks who wanted to kill him. Can anything be more wrong than that?

Judas felt sorry about what he did to Jesus, but it didn't help. That's because he tried to make it all right himself instead of asking God to forgive him. He was dead wrong this time.

When you do something wrong, you make it worse if you don't pray to God for forgiveness.

Think of something you did wrong today. Ask God to forgive you. How do you feel?

IMPORTANT STUFF

Read Matthew 6:31-34.

Put God's kingdom first in your life.

Marty Lyons figured his new head coach didn't really know what was important in life.

As a freshman, Lyons sat in his first meeting with head coach Bear Bryant in the summer of 1975. He couldn't believe what he heard.

The Bear said there were four things he wanted his players to do while they were at Alabama. First was be proud of your family. Second was be proud of your religion. Third was get an education. Fourth was try to win some football games.

Lyons thought that was nuts. He figured the most important thing of all was winning football games. He later found out, though, that he didn't really know what was important.

He was an All-SEC defensive tackle in 1977 and All-America in 1978. He went on to have

Crimson Tide

a great career in the NFL.

Along the way, Lyons learned that if he kept what was important to him in the order that Coach Bear Bryant had said, then good things would happen to him.

A priority is what you regard as what's most important in your life. It's what really matters to you. It may not be football as Marty Lyons thought it was, but it's something.

It could be anything, from making good grades to being a cheerleader one day to getting to a new level on a video game. It may even be making your parents proud of you.

The big question is whether God is one of your priorities. The truth is he should be first. God said we are to seek him first. Not second or third but first.

In Jesus, God showed you the way you are to do everything. You serve and obey him.

God — and God alone — is No. 1.

Write down ten things that are important to you. Where is God on that list? Talk about how important God is to you.

CHOW DOWN

Read Genesis 9:1-3.

I now give you everything that lives and moves to eat.

Before a big game, one Tide player wasn't really worried. Except about hot tamales.

Millard "Dixie" Howell was an All-American halfback in 1934. He is in the College Football Hall of Fame.

On Jan. 1, 1935, the Crimson Tide won its fourth national title by beating Stanford 29-13 in the Rose Bowl. Howell had the best game of his career and was the star.

That's kind of funny because leading up to the game, he wasn't thinking a whole lot about football. Instead, his mind was on hot tamales.

It seems that while he was in California for the game, Howell got a real craving for the Mexican dish. He said that after the game he was going to eat six of them. He liked them so much that he even dreamed about them.

Howell said that his head coach wouldn't let the players eat tamales before the game. "But as soon as that game is over — well, you watch," he said.

Americans really do love food, even tamales. We love to eat all sorts of different things, from hamburgers to chicken, pizza to ice cream. We even have TV channels that talk about food all the time. They show people how to make new dishes for their family to try and eat.

Food is one of God's really good ideas. Isn't it amazing to think that from one apple seed, an entire tree full of apples can grow and give you apples year after year?

God created this system that lets all living things grow and nourish one another. Your food comes from God and nowhere else. The least you can do is thank him for it.

Three questions to answer: What's your favorite food? What can you cook? Do you thank God before you eat?

A SURE THING

Read Romans 8:28-30.

Those whom God calls for his purposes will be saved.

Tennessee's kick was a sure thing. Alabama would lose.

The Tide was undefeated and headed for the SEC championship and maybe the national title in 2009. But the Bama-Tennessee game is so famous that it is known as the Third Saturday in October. It's a hard game to win.

Alabama led 12-3 with only 6:31 left in the game. The Tide's win was a sure thing. Then everything went wrong. Bama fumbled and UT got the ball and scored. It was 12-10.

And then Tennessee got the ball with an on-side kick. That's a kickoff that goes only a short distance where it can be recovered by the kicking team. Tennessee moved to the Alabama 27-yard line with four seconds left.

Crimson Tide

A field goal would win the game for UT. "We just knew we were going to win," said a Tennessee player.

But Alabama lineman Terrence Cody, a two-time All-America, reached up and blocked the kick. Finally, Bama's win was a sure thing.

You never know if Alabama or your school team is going to win until they play the game, do you? Just like you never know what is going to happen tomorrow. You may expect to be going to school, but something could happen.

Life is like that for kids and for grown-ups. You think you know what's going to happen, but you can never really be sure.

Faith in Jesus is different. It's true that you can't know what will happen tomorrow afternoon or the next day. But with Jesus, you can know for sure what will happen forever.

That's because your future is in God's hands, and that's a sure thing.

List some things you are sure of. Then list ways something could happen to them. Can anything take God from you?

ALIVE AGAIN

Read Matthew 28:1-9.

The angel said, "Jesus is not here. He has risen just like he said he would."

Alabama's basketball season was dead and buried. Over. Then resurrection came.

"It felt like a funeral," said one writer after the Bama men lost to Ole Miss in January of 2006. The Rebels were so bad that they were in last place in the league, but they had beaten Alabama. The Tide wanted to make the NCAA Tournament, but the chances were now slim.

Not only had the Tide lost the game, they had lost one of their best players, Chuck Davis, with a knee injury. Head coach Mark Gottfried had only seven players left to play. All that was left was a long, painful season.

But Coach Gottfried refused to give up. He said his guys had to find a way to resurrect their season. And they did just that! They won six of their next eight games and finished the season with a 17-12 record.

On March 12, they watched on TV for the tournament teams to be named. They were one of them. They had resurrected the season.

A resurrection happens when someone who was dead is alive again. Of course, nobody on the Alabama team of 2005-06 was really dead. In sports, announcers often speak of a team being resurrected. That means it wound up with a pretty good season after it had started off badly. Like Alabama did.

Resurrections do occur in the Bible, but one stands alone. All others are just resuscitations like when an ambulance crew helps somebody stay alive. The person will still die one day.

But when Jesus was resurrected on the first Easter, he was alive forever. And that's the way it will be for you one day. If you believe that Jesus is your savior, you will live forever.

Name some people you know who are in Heaven. Are you sad they're gone? Are you happy you'll see them in heaven?

TEARS IN HEAVEN

Read Revelation 21:1-4.

There will be no more death, grief, crying, or pain.

Bear Bryant figured it had been twenty or thirty years since he had cried. So what in the world could make him get all choked up?

In 1965, a writer saw the Alabama legend looking teary-eyed in a hotel room. He asked what was wrong with the Bama boss. "He just lost an assistant coach," a friend answered.

"How old was he?" asked the writer. "Twenty-nine," was the answer. The writer was horrified. "That's awfully young! How did he die?" "Oh, he didn't die," his friend said. "He just went to Texas A&M."

Bear Bryant shed his tears because Gene Stallings had taken the job as A&M's head football coach and athletic director.

Stallings came back to Tuscaloosa in 1980

as the Alabama head coach. He won 70 games in seven seasons, including the 1992 national championship.

But as a tearful Bear Bryant said, he cried because he was happy for Stallings and his new job but he was sad he was losing him.

Did you cry any today? Crying is just part of growing up. Like the last time you fell and had to have stitches. Or that time you ran your bike into a ditch and wrecked it.

It may surprise you to learn that grown-ups — even tough ones like Bear Bryant — cry, too. Tears and sadness are just a part of life.

But have you ever cried tears of joy? Like one time when Alabama won a game. Or how about the day when you were baptized?

If there are tears in Heaven, they'll be tears of joy, not sadness. Think about it. If you cry when Alabama wins, don't you think you'll cry when you finally see Jesus face to face?

Read Revelation 21:4 again.
What things will not be in heaven?
How does that make you feel?

THE ANSWER

Read Colossians 2:2-4.

You will understand the mystery of God, which is in Christ Jesus.

Jeremiah Castille admitted he was a bad kid headed down the wrong road. Then he found the answer one summer night right in his own neighborhood.

Castille was an All-American defensive back in 1982. He was so close to Bear Bryant that he was a pallbearer at the coach's funeral. He became an ordained minister and the Alabama team chaplain.

It wasn't always that way for him, however. Growing up, his family wasn't a good one. His mom and dad fought and drank alcohol.

Living in that environment, Castille got into trouble. Before he was out of the eighth grade, he had been expelled for fighting. "I was just doing what I had learned at home," he said.

But the summer after he was expelled, he went to a revival down the street from his home. There, he met Jesus and gave his life to a personal relationship with his savior.

Jeremiah Castille had found the answer he had been searching for. His life has never been the same since that night.

You ask a lot of questions and get a lot of answers in school, don't you? It's the same when you play a sport or even a video game; you need answers to learn how to play.

You will look for a lot of answers as you grow up, go to high school, graduate, go to college, and then become an adult. The questions will change as your life changes.

No answers are more important than your search for God and what he wants you to do with your life. Like everything else, the questions will change as you do. The answer for your life, however, is always Jesus.

Write down some questions you'd like God to answer. How do you get answers from God about your life?

THE BLUSH

Read John 2:1-11.

Jesus' mother told him they had run out of wine at the wedding.

Alabama once had a running back whose nickname embarrassed him no end.

Johnny Musso was an All-America in 1970. From 1969-71, he set a school record at the time for most yards rushing. The Tide sports information director decided the team's star needed a flashy nickname for publicity. He set about trying to come up with one.

Musso said they tried several things and they all "went from bad to worse." One of the worst was Johnny "GoGo" Musso.

When the sophomore showed up for the pre-game meal for the first game of 1969, other players started laughing at him and making noises like a horse. That's because his new nickname was in the newspapers that morning.

Crimson Tide

Johnny Musso was the Italian Stallion.

That nickname may have made it into the movies. After he left Alabama, Musso played football in Canada with Carl Weathers, who later became an actor. He played Apollo Creed in the *Rocky* movies where Rocky Balboa was known as the Italian Stallion.

Ever come up with answer in class so wrong that everybody laughed? Ever stumbled over your own feet right in front of your friends? Man, that's embarrassing!

Embarrassment helps sometimes because it teaches us not to do that again. Too many of us, though, are embarrassed by our faith. We won't claim the name of Jesus in public.

Here's the awful flip side. If you're embarrassed by Jesus, he's embarrassed by you. That means that when you appear before God one day, Jesus won't know you to save you.

That's not embarrassing. That's horrible.

Is there anything about Jesus that embarrasses you? Why? Come up with ways to get rid of it.

UNBELIEVABLE!

Read Hebrews 3:12-14.

Do not have an unbelieving heart that turns you away from God.

Alabama's George Linn once made what is maybe the most unbelievable shot in college basketball history.

In 1955, the Tide romped past North Carolina 77-55. As the first half was about to end, Linn, a junior forward, pulled down a rebound. He turned and threw the ball as hard and as far as he could. It sailed 84 feet 11 inches. And hit nothing but net.

Teammate Jerry Harper said the place got real quiet at first. "You could hear a pin drop for the longest time. Then it sure enough broke loose." Another Alabama player, Leon Marlaire, said it was just like throwing a touchdown pass. "It never touched the rim," he said.

The North Carolina coach got down on his

hands and knees and marked the spot on the court. He said it was the longest shot ever. A metal marker was inserted into the floor to remember Linn's unbelievable shot.

No visual record remains of it. In those days, the Alabama athletic department filmed only SEC games at home.

You know, it doesn't really matter that you don't believe in some things. Like magic. Or that a horseshoe can being you good luck if you nail it over your door.

But it matters a whole lot that you believe in Jesus as the Son of God. Some people say that Jesus was a good man and a good teacher and that's all.

They are wrong, and their unbelief is bad for them. God doesn't fool around with people who don't believe in Jesus as their Savior. He locks them out of Heaven forever.

If you believe, you'll go to Heaven one day and be happy with God and Jesus.

Talk to your parents about some things you don't believe in and why you don't.

THE SIMPLE LIFE

Read 1 John 1:5-10.

If we admit to God that we have sinned, he will forgive us.

Football looks complicated, but when Bama beat Clemson in 2008, it was pretty simple.

The game was the season opener. Head coach Nick Saban knew what simple formula Alabama should use to win. "Our defensive line is going to have to whip their offensive line," he said. When the game was over, Clemson's head coach was wailing that "we got whipped about every way you can get whipped."

That's because the Tide buried the Tigers 34-10. And it wasn't that close.

The game was supposed to be a really good one. Clemson had some big stars, so everybody figured they'd give Alabama fits.

Yeah, right. They didn't know about Coach Saban's simple formula. Clemson couldn't run the ball against Bama's line. They had only 70 yards in the first half.

The simple formula worked in the last half, too. Clemson's only points came on a kickoff return. They wound up with zero yards rushing for the game.

Alabama's line beat Clemson's line. It was that simple.

Being a kid isn't simple. You have to juggle school and homework, baseball or basketball, church and Sunday school, dancing class, 4-H, and anything else that comes along. You have to do your chores at the house like making up your bed and taking out the garbage.

But, you know, life is really pretty simple. Just like Alabama showed Clemson. Put the basic stuff first. Worship God, love your family, honor your teachers, and always do your best.

That's means you're obeying God in the way you live. It's simple — and it's the best.

It's simple: Ask God for forgiveness of our sins and you get it. Why do you think God made it so easy?

AS A RULE

Read Luke 5:27-32.

Some religious leaders complained because Jesus ate with sinners.

A really strange rule helped Alabama score a touchdown on their way to the national title.

The Tide played Stanford in the 1935 Rose Bowl for the national championship. Alabama was a passing team with its great wide receiver Don Hutson. He was so good that he changed the way the college game was played; a lot of teams started throwing the ball.

But when halfback Dixie Howell got hurt against Stanford, Alabama had to run the ball. Howell was the one who threw the ball to Hutson. The coach sent Hutson into the game and told him to call a set of running plays.

But a strange rule meant Hutson couldn't say anything in the huddle until the first play was over. He couldn't even tell everyone the coach's play! The quarterback smartly figured the coach wanted a pass to Hutson.

So he sent Hutson long and threw him a 50-yard bomb for a touchdown. Alabama was on its way to a 29-13 win and the national title. Helped by a strange rule.

You live with a whole set of rules, don't you? Go to bed at a certain time. Don't play in the street. Don't act ugly to your brother or sister. Be polite to your teachers. Make up your bed.

Rules are hard but they aren't always bad things. Without them, our whole world and our country would be a mess. Nobody would get along, and people couldn't do stuff together.

The rules Jesus didn't like were those that said some people should be treated badly. He broke them, and he expects you to do it, too. You should never mistreat anybody because somebody else says it's the thing to do.

Jesus loves that person. So should you.

Think of a rule that you don't like.
Why do you think you have it?
What would happen if you broke it?

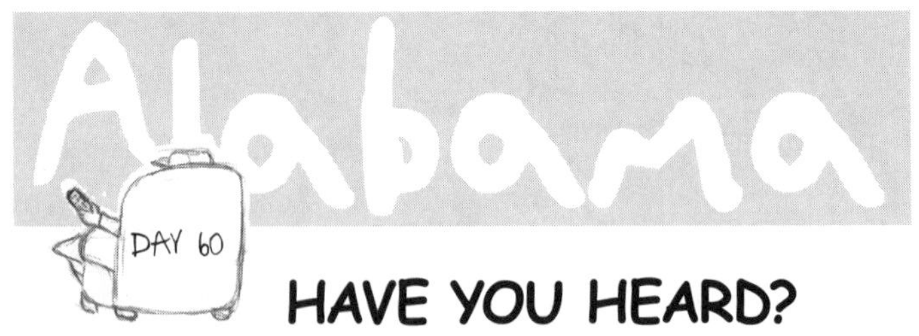

HAVE YOU HEARD?

Mark 1:21-28.

News about Jesus spread quickly.

If you like watching college football on TV at night, you have Alabama to thank for it.

Once, the TV networks thought football was just for the days. Then in October 1969, ABC decided to try a night game for the first time ever. They picked Alabama and Ole Miss. The game was supposed to start at 8 but had to wait for Lawrence Welk to get over. (Have your parents tell you who Lawrence Welk was.)

If the game was a bad one, college football probably wouldn't be on at night for a while. The first half was pretty boring, too. ABC's big bosses were nervous they had tried something that had failed.

Then came the last half. Archie Manning of Ole Miss went wild and set an all-time college record for yards passing in a game. Alabama quarterback Scott Hunter had a good night also; he set an Alabama record for passing yards in a game.

Alabama won 35-32 in one of the greatest games of all time. Never again would college football have to wait for Lawrence Welk. The word was out: College football was fun!

Man, commercials are everywhere, aren't they? You can't escape them. Chances are your shirt has a company logo on it. That means you're a commercial with feet!

Jesus was pretty good at advertising also. He just didn't have TV or the Internet. All he had was word of mouth. All he could do was talk to people, and that's what he did. Jesus went from town to town preaching, teaching, and talking to people.

Almost two thousand years later, nothing has really changed. Talking to someone else about Jesus is still the best way to get the word out about the savior of the world.

When was the last time you told someone about Jesus? It's time to do it again.

LOST AND FOUND

Read Luke 15:11-24.

The father said, "My son was lost, and now he's found."

Michael Thompson lost his home, his car, and his golf scholarship. He found a better life.

Thompson was a star for two years on the Tulane golf team in New Orleans. He was quite happy as the 2005-06 season neared. Then overnight, he lost everything about his life as he knew it — to Hurricane Katrina.

When he left his apartment to find safety from the storm, Thompson thought he would be back in a few days. He dropped his car off at a body shop and even took his golf clubs with him. Of course, it wasn't a vacation at all but a major tragedy.

Thompson never did see his car again. After the flood, Tulane dropped its golf program. He had to look for a new college.

Crimson Tide

He found a home at Alabama. He was All-America in 2008 and led the Tide to its first SEC championship in 29 years. "It's been a wild ride," Thompson said about the life he lost and the one he found.

Everybody loses things. Why is it that when you lose something, it's always in the last place you look?

Have you ever heard the preacher talk about people being lost? He's not saying they need help from their GPS to find their way home from church.

When Christians talk about someone who is lost, they are speaking of people who don't know Jesus; they aren't saved. They are lost because they haven't found the only way to Heaven — through faith in Jesus.

God never leaves the lost; they leave him. And Jesus is always ready with open arms to welcome the lost people home.

Since you were born, Jesus has been looking for you. Has he found you? Do you know someone who's lost?

BEST FRIEND

Read Ecclesiastes 4:9-12.

If someone falls down, his friend can help him up.

Because Kevin Jackson had a friend, Alabama kept an All-American safety.

In Sept. 1995, Jackson was ready to pack up and leave Tuscaloosa. He had been benched for the Arkansas game and was feeling pretty bad. He had talked to the coaches at Samford University about transferring there. "I just felt I wasn't needed at Alabama," he said.

Darrell Blackburn was Jackson's roommate and friend. He saw what was going on. When Jackson tried to leave the dorm, Blackburn got in his way and took his car keys away. "You're not quitting," he said.

Jackson's friend led him back inside where they sat down and talked it over. Blackburn told his friend to stick it out, that his turn would come. It did indeed. Jackson was All-America as a senior.

The friend who saved his career wasn't on the field with him, however. Blackburn had to give up football because of kidney problems.

God wired us for friendship. We like people. God calls us to mingle among his people, not to stay by ourselves. The Bible says friendship makes you stronger. A friend can help you up when you fall, keep you warm on a cold night on a camping trip, and stand up for you when somebody else calls you a bad name.

Even Jesus had friends. His closest friends were the twelve disciples. They went with him everywhere, ran errands for him, and helped him when he was tired.

Most of us would do almost anything for a friend. But would you tell a friend about Jesus? That's the best thing of all you can do for a person who is your friend.

Draw up a list of your friends. Do all of them know Jesus? If not, what can you as their friend do about it?

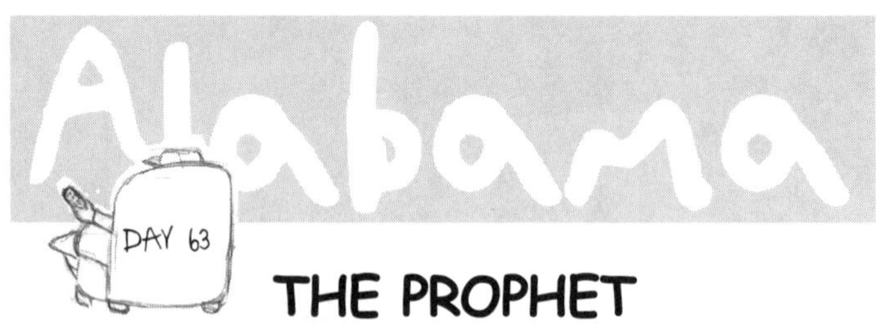

THE PROPHET

Isaiah 53:6-9.

He went like a lamb to the slaughter and said not a word.

"In 1961 it became official. Bear Bryant was a prophet."

We think prophets are weird people who can predict the future. So what made the great coach look like a prophet in 1961?

Well, it all went back to the first meeting he had as Alabama's head football coach in 1958. He told the players if they worked and dedicated themselves, they would be national champions in four years. Freshman Billy Neighbors said he thought the man was crazy.

Why was that prediction so far-fetched? The Tide had won only four games in three years.

But it got better that first year: 5-4-1. Then came a 7-2-2 record in 1959 followed by an 8-1-2 record in 1960.

Crimson Tide

And then came 1961, which was the fourth season that the Bear had talked about at that first meeting. What happened then?

It turned out the Bear knew what he was talking about. Alabama went undefeated and won the national championship.

In the Old Testament, you read a lot about God's prophets. Isaiah was one. Did these guys walk around acting funny and predicting the future? Not really.

Instead, they delivered a word that God had given them. Sometimes — as when Isaiah spoke of Jesus' suffering and death — that involved the future. But typically, the prophets told all the people what God wanted them to do, how God said they should live.

Where is your prophet? How can you find out what God wants you to do? You read the Bible and you pray. It's all right there for you.

Make ten predictions (like how many games Alabama will win this year); write them down. Check them later to see how many you got right.

GOOD LUCK

Read 1 Samuel 28:7-8, 11-14.

Saul said, "Find me a woman who can talk to the dead, so I can ask her some questions."

Antoine Pettway wasn't superstitious, but he was glad to have those ugly red shoes back.

The point guard wore a pair of hideous ruby red basketball sneakers during the 2001-02 season. The Tide won the SEC championship. He retired them only because they wore out.

After Alabama upset Stanford in the 2004 NCAA Tournament, Pettway started thinking about those ugly red shoes and the good luck they had brought him.

Someone in the Tide basketball offices had put a pair of them back just in case Pettway ever wanted them. Teammate Earnest Shelton said that with his red shoes, Pettway might "come out and have a monster game now."

Crimson Tide

He did. The shoes didn't have anything to do with it, but against Syracuse, Pettway scored ten points, had nine assists, and didn't have a single turnover. The Tide upset the defending national champs.

Most everybody is at least a little bit superstitious. They'll knock on wood or won't walk under a ladder. A rabbit's foot may be good luck, but if it's on a key chain, it wasn't very lucky for the rabbit.

Have you ever seen one of those signs by the road with a picture of a hand on it? It may say "Palm Reader." That's sort of the person King Saul went to for advice.

The problem was that God had told Saul not to do that. He tells you the same thing. Why? What's the harm? If you do that, then you're trusting in people and not God.

Even if you're not superstitious, you trust in and rely on something. It should be God — and God alone.

What superstition do you have?
Superstition is silly, so why is it bad?

STORM WARNING

Luke 12:4-10.

If you reject Jesus on Earth,
God will reject you in Heaven.

Don't go! Don't go in there!" With those scary words, senior end Baxter Booth warned his teammates.

In 1957, the Alabama football players knew that their new coach, Bear Bryant, was tough. They had no idea how tough.

It started with the very first workout. The players went into the closed wrestling room by position. Those waiting to go in sat around in sweats. No one knew what was happening.

And then Booth came out. He had blood running out of his nose and an ear. He had vomit all down the front of his sweatshirt. That was shocking enough, but then he yelled out, "Don't go! Don't go in there! They'll kill you! Don't go in that room!"

Crimson Tide

They had been warned, but still the uneasy players went in anyway. They had to see what was going on. They all came out the same way Booth had: covered in their own blood and vomit after the toughest workout any of them had ever had. But they had been warned.

What do flashing lights and clanging bells at a railroad crossing warn you of? What about a message that scrolls across your TV set when it's raining outside?

You get lots of warnings in life. They tell you to be alert for danger, for something that may hurt you. You pay attention to them or ignore them based on whether or not you think you stand a good chance of getting hurt.

Jesus issued a warning nobody should ever ignore. He told you to claim him as your Lord and Savior in life and be claimed by God in Heaven. Reject him and be banned from Heaven. It's that simple. And that dangerous.

Have you ever warned somebody about something? Why did you do it? Why did Jesus warn us?

THE SUB

Read Galatians 3:10-14.

Christ took your punishment for your sins upon himself by dying on the cross.

In one of the most important games in Alabama basketball history, the subs refused to play.

In the 1950s, Kentucky ruled college basketball and especially the SEC. But when Alabama and UK met in February 1956, the Tide was 10-0 and Kentucky was 10-1 in the conference.

Three minutes into the second half, Kentucky led 51-50. Then something happened that Alabama basketball fans will never forget. Over the next seven minutes, Alabama outscored Kentucky 28-1 and led 78-52!

The Alabama gym went wild as the team kept on scoring points. Into the 80s. And the 90s. The head coach finally decided to pull his starters and let everyone take part in the fun. But the subs wouldn't go in!

Why in the world? They wanted to reach 100 points. So the starters played on. Alabama won 101-77. The Tide thus became the first team in history to score one hundred points on Kentucky.

Man, wouldn't life be great if you had a sub to take care of things for you? Like take your tests. Take out the garbage. Brush your teeth.

But did you know that you do have a sub for all matters of life and death? God demands a sacrifice to get us right with him after we sin. A sin is anything that angers God.

Once upon a time, that sacrifice meant animals like pigeons and goats. But when was the last time you burned an animal in your church? Why don't you have to do that anymore? How do you stay right with God?

You have a sub in Jesus. He made the sacrifice for all time when he died on the cross.

What would happen if you set fire to a goat in your church?

A LONG SHOT

Read Matthew 9:9-10.

Jesus said, "Follow me," and Matthew got up and did it.

How shabby is a softball team with no batting cage, no equipment shed, and no home field! And this bunch was going to make the College World Series? You're joking, right?

That was the situation in 2000 when the Alabama softball program started its fourth season. They got their first batting cage that year. They also got their first home stadium that year; they had played their home games at recreation parks. The equipment shed was the trunk and back seat of head coach Patrick Murphy's car.

Alabama was a very long shot to make the softball world series. But they did it by upsetting powerhouse Arizona State. "The reporters in Arizona couldn't believe it," Murphy said.

Neither could anybody else. But there they were. The long shots from Alabama that didn't even have an equipment shed had made it to the Women's College World Series.

A long shot is someone or some team that doesn't stand a good chance of doing something. You're probably a real long shot to get married this year or to be named Bama's head football coach.

Matthew was a long shot to be one of Jesus' close friends. He was a tax collector, which meant he was a real bad man. He got rich by bullying and stealing from his own people, his own neighbors.

Yet, Jesus said only two words to this low-life: "Follow me." And Matthew did it.

Like Matthew, we're all long shots to get to Heaven because we can't stand before God with pure, clean hearts. Not unless we do what Matthew did: Get up and follow Jesus.

Name five things that are long shots in your life (like becoming president). Then name five things that are sure shots (like going to bed tonight).

WHO, ME?

Read Judges 6:12-16.

"Lord," Gideon asked, "how can I save Israel? I'm a nobody even in my own family."

Steve Sloan was minding his own business, reading the newspaper, and got a big surprise! Right in the paper it said he was Alabama's starting quarterback for the Sugar Bowl.

Sloan was an All-American quarterback who led the Tide to two SEC and two national titles. In 1963, though, he was a sophomore who started as a defensive back. He was the third-string quarterback and didn't expect to play at all in the bowl game except on defense.

When the starter got in trouble with Coach Bear Bryant and was suspended for the bowl game, Sloan figured the second-string quarterback would start. But Coach Bryant picked him, though he had never started a game in

Crimson Tide

college at quarterback. Sloan didn't even hear about it from the coaches; he found out when he read it in the paper!

In the game, the coaches forgot that Sloan was a starter on defense. He wound up playing both quarterback and defensive back the whole first half. Alabama won 12-7.

You ever said, "Who, me?" Maybe when the teacher called on you in class? Or when somebody asked you to sing a solo? Your stomach kind of knots up, doesn't it? You get real nervous, too.

That's the way Gideon felt when God called on him to lead his people in battle. And you might feel the same way when somebody calls on you to say a prayer. Or to read a part in Sunday school.

Hey, I can't do that, you might say. But you can. God wants you to do stuff for him. Like Gideon, God thinks you can do it just fine. And with God's help, you will. Just like Gideon.

Think of some ways you can help at Sunday school. And then volunteer.

PAYBACK

Read Matthew 5:38-45.

Jesus said to love those who don't like you and to pray for those who do you wrong.

Alabama players waited a year to get their revenge, but they got it in fine fashion.

The SEC championship game of 2008 was really painful for Alabama fans. The Tide led Florida 20-17 in the last quarter but lost 31-20. The Gators then went on to win the national title that the Tide could have won.

"It wasn't going to happen again," said left guard Mike Johnson. "We had a hunger." He said that right before the same two teams met in the 2009 SEC championship game. The Tide wanted to pay Florida back for what had happened the year before.

From the opening snap, Bama dominated. The Tide never let up and trounced the Gators and Tim Tebow 32-13. Tide quarterback Greg McElroy was the game's MVP.

Florida trailed only 19-13 at halftime. This time, though, there would be no last-quarter comeback. The Tide had its sweet payback — and went on to win the national title.

In a big rivalry like the Iron Bowl, one team is always looking for payback from getting beat the year before. It's part of what makes college football so much fun.

But real life doesn't work that way. Should you get even when somebody does something wrong to you? Jesus said not to.

The reason is that paying somebody back only makes everything worse. It will make the other person want to pay you back and hurt you again. And so it keeps going. It's just a mess when you live like that.

Jesus said to do something much easier. Just forget it. Go on about your business. Go on with your life. It's more fun that way.

Talk to your parents about something wrong someone has done to you. What should you do about it?

THE GREATEST

Read Mark 9:33-37.

To be the greatest in God's kingdom, you must put others above yourself and serve them.

More than thirty years after it happened, it is still regarded by many Alabama fans as the greatest play in the school's football history.

On Jan. 1, 1979, Alabama played Penn State in the Sugar Bowl for the national championship. Alabama led 14-7 in the fourth quarter, but Penn State moved to within inches of the Tide goal line on fourth down.

The Alabama coaches figured Penn State would try to power the ball in. They were right.

On the field for Alabama was Barry Krauss, a senior linebacker. He was a two-time All-America. When Penn State snapped the ball, the runner tried to leap over a pile in the middle of the field. Krauss met him face mask to face mask. He hit the runner so hard that he broke his helmet. But State did not score.

With the greatest play in its history, the Tide had stopped Penn State inches from a touchdown. Alabama won the game 14-7.

When you think about being the greatest at something, what do you think of? Probably being better than everybody else, right? You get the highest score on a video game or on a test. You win at tennis. You build the greatest thing of all with your Legos.

But Jesus turned being the greatest upside down. He said something really strange. To be the greatest for Jesus, you have to be last. How weird is that? What he meant is that you must put other people first in your life. You always are kind to and help other people.

When you live like that, God is so pleased with you that he names you one of his children. You can't be any greater than that!

Promise yourself that at school you will seek somebody out to smile at them and help them.

NOTES

(by devotion number)

1 In one game against . . . the game was over.: Clyde Bolton, *The Crimson Tide* (Huntsville: The Strode Publishers, 1972), p. 31.

2 An ESPN announcer said . . . to do its best.: Gene Wojciechowski, "Tide at Pinnacle of College Football," *ESPN.com*, Jan. 7, 2013, http://www.espn.go.com/college-football/bowls.

3 Bama guard Mykal Riley . . . hit this shot": Thomas Lake, "The Shot That Saved Lives," *Sports Illustrated*, March 16, 2009, http://www.sportsillustrated.cnn.com/vault/article/magazine/MAG153064/index.htm.

3 During the extra time, . . . in the building were safe: Lake.

4 He sent a freshman . . . over a month.: Gentry Estes, "Hope Is Alive," *The Mobile Press-Register*, May 31, 2009, http://www.al.com/alabamabaseball/mobileregister/women.ssf?/base/sports.

7 They made the funny . . . were really friendly.: Al Browning, *Third Saturday in October* (Nashville: Cumberland House Publishing, Inc., 2001), p. 143.

8 "simply the best there ever was.": Mike Puma, "Bear Bryant 'Simply the Best There Ever Was,'" *ESPN*, http://espn.go.com/classic/biography/s/Bryant_Bear.html.

8 He can look . . . "Love Lifted Me.": Frank Deford, "I Do Love the Football," *Sports Illustrated*, Nov. 23, 1981, http://www.sportsillustrated.cnn.com/vault/article/magazine/MAG1125024/index.html.

9 the Tide head coach . . . stomped on an orange.: Jerry Kirshenbaum, "High Tide Washes over Vols," *Sports Illustrated*, Feb. 13,1978, http://www.sportsillustrated.cnn.com/vault/article/magazine/MAG1093316/index.htm.

10 Billboards welcomed the new . . . Tuscaloosa in 1958.: Eli Gold, *Crimson Nation* (Nashville: Rutledge Hill Press, 2005), p. 91.

10 He told some rich . . . he locked the gates.: Gold.

11 Charley Boswell was in a . . . him to play golf.: "Blind Golfer 'Reads' the Greens," *The Palm Beach Post*, March 1, 1971, http://www.news.google.com/newspapers?nid=1964&dat=19710301.

11 On a golf course, . . . middle of the fairway.:"Charles A. Boswell," *Encyclopedia of Alabama*, http://www.encyclopediaofalabama.org/face/Article.jsp?id=h-1771.

12 It had a balcony . . . had to miss a game.: Clyde Bolton, *The Basketball Tide* (Huntsville: The Strode Publishers, 1977), pp. 53-54.

13 He even moved into . . . to try the Wishbone.: Gold, p. 143.

14 The Crimson Tide leader . . . want to play better.: Gold, p. 202.

15 "We were right there,": "#2 Alabama 20 -- #22 South Carolina 6," *Yea Alabama* (Hanover, Mass.: Maple Street Press LLC, 2010), p. 40.

15 He said he thought . . . he was so tired.: "#2 Alabama 20," p. 38.

17 "It's not something that's a one-time thing,": Ian R. Rapoport, "Turning Points," *The Birmingham News*, Dec. 2, 2008, p. 1-C.

17 "We needed to make a change,": Rapoport, "Turning Points."

18 All winter long, . . . for playing time.: Rapoport, "Turning Points."
18 Don grew up on . . . looking right at them.: Scott, pp. 151-52.
19 He once said that . . . screamed out, "War Eagle!": Ray Kennedy, "Battle for Braggin' Rights," *Sports Illustrated*, Dec. 9, 1974, http:/www.sports illustrated.cnn.com/vault/article/magazine/MAG1089323/index.htm.
20 The ceiling of the gym . . . bounced to the floor!: Bolton, *The Basketball Tide*, p. 26.
20 One time in 1916, . . . concert on time!: Bolton, *The Basketball Tide*, p. 33.
21 Coach Bryant said Namath . . . coach I ever knew.": "Joe Namath," *Wikipedia, the free encyclopedia*, http://www.en.wikipedia.org/wiki/Joe_Namath.
21 Mad at himself, he . . . act like a show-off.": Gold, p. 124.
22 He thought Coach Bryant . . . straightened out real fast.": Scott, p. 82.
23 They noticed right off . . . each other a hug.": Steve Kirk, "Tide Coach Embraces Slap-Hitting Speedster," *The Birmingham News*, May 10, 2006, p. 1-C.
24 for one hour each . . . tipped it at his players.: Don Wade, *Always Alabama* (New York: Simon & Schuster, 2006), p. 140.
25 In high school, Todd . . . helped anyone else, either.": Tommy Hicks, *Game of My Life: Alabama* (Champaign, Il.: Sports Publishing L.L.C., 2006), p. 90.
26 Rader called a run . . . threw a touchdown pass: Steve Kirk, "Not Like They Drew It Up," *The Birmingham News*, Sept. 25, 2005, p. 1-C.
27 "I saw some green and I ran to it,": Doug Segrest, "Bama Sacks Michigan," *The Birmingham News*, Jan. 2, 1997, p. 01-C.
28 Sports Illustrated called former . . . lineman of all time": Scott, p. 129.
28 His first year a writer . . . the last three years.": Scott, p. 129.
29 "The bottom line was that things were bad,": Gold, p. 88.
29 I came here to make Alabama a winner again,": Gold, p. 91.
29 He said the first . . . his players were winners.: Scott, p. 19.
29 At the first practice, . . . garbage pails for vomiting.: Scott, p. 18.
29 "No college football coach . . . better than Bryant.": Scott, p. 16.
30 Before the season started, . . . died after being kidnapped.: Mark Beech, "The Tide Has Turned," *Sports Illustrated*, Oct. 10, 2005, http://www.sportsillustrated.cnn.com/vault/article/magazine/MAG1103865/index.htm.
30 In the last minutes . . . had come to town.: Beech.
31 SEC basketball coaches were . . . a "home-cooked rat.": Curry Kirkpatrick, "Solution to a Thorny Problem," *Sports Illustrated*, March 15, 1982, http://www.sportsillustrated.cnn.com/vault/article/magazine/MAG1125307/index.htm.
32 Bear Bryant said he could even sell tickets.: Hicks, p. 37.
32 Ray was all set to . . . to play for Alabama.: Hicks, p. 44.
32 "I didn't care where I played just as long as I was playing," Hicks, p. 46.
33 "I jumped up and patted . . . and celebrated too.": Hicks, p. 125.
33 A book published years . . . 13th greatest play.: Hicks, p. 126.
34 A high-school teammate and . . . would have gone there.: Hicks, p. 106.
35 "When Coach Bryant stepped . . . on the first play.: Gold, p. 137.
36 The team visited Kimbrough . . . made with his teammates.: Bolton, *The Basketball Tide*, p. 61.

37 His teammates were the . . . won the national title.: Andy Staples, "Ingram Won Heisman, " *SI.com*, Jan. 5, 2010, http://www.sportsillustrated.cnn.com/2010/writers/andy_staples/01/04/rolando-mcclain/index.htm.
38 "Four-zero-zero." . . . all over his apartment.: Ray Melick, "A Serious Miler," *The Birmingham News*, May 28, 2009, p. 1-C.
38 Right before the SEC . . . mile race in 3:59:4.: Melick.
39 Phillips couldn't sleep at . . . him to play quarterback. Wayne Atcheson, *Faith of the Crimson Tide* (Grand Island, Neb.: Cross Training Publishing, 2000), p. 210.
39 As Phillips walked toward . . . wanted him to make.: Atcheson, p. 211.
40 In 1958, the Bear . . . to be nice to people.: "Bear Bryant Knew How to Be Nice," *Redelephants.com*, http://www.redelephants.com/CoachBearBryant.html.
41 In June 2007, Wells suddenly . . . it meant to him.: Ian R. Rapoport, "Apologetic Wells Returns as Coach," *The Birmingham News*, June 28, 2007, p. 1-B.
42 Dwight decided he would . . . he wasn't ready.: Scott, p. 158.
42 he decided to go to . . . signed with the Tide.: Scott, p. 159.
43 The crowd went silent . . . "He did it!": Dick Heller, "Refs Didn't Cotton to Off-Bench Stop," *The Washington Times*, Jan. 1, 2007, http://www.ricefootball.net/collegeinnwtstory.htm.
43 After the game, Lewis . . . runner he had tackled.: Wade, p. 4
43 "I don't know what got into me,": Heller.
44 Tide players celebrated on . . . into the locker room.: Doug Segrest, "Beatdown in T-Town," *The birmingham News*, Nov. 30, 2008, p. 3-C.
44 Safety Rashad Johnson said . . . a little victory jig.: Segrest, Beatdown in T-Town."
45 With only 7:42 left . . . going to win the game.: Steve Irvine, "One Is Done," *The Birmingham News*, March 21, 2004, p. 1-C.
45 That's when Gottfried . . . last 1:33 of the game.: Irvine, "One Is Done."
46 they saw themselves as . . . got practice this week,": Austin Murphy, "A Tidy Finish, *Sports Illustrated*, Dec. 14, 1992, http://www.sportsillustrated.cnn.com/vault/article/magazine/MAG1004647/index.htm.
47 "a thinker, one of . . . from the East.: Bolton, *The Crimson Tide*, p. 57.
48 He figured that anything . . . as loud as he could.: Bolton, *The Basketball Tide*, p. 96.
48 One newspaper said Crews . . . was "a sight.": Bolton, *The Basketball Tide*, p. 97.
49 The Bear had once . . . national titles instead.: Peter Holiday, "On the Mark," *Yea Alabama 2009* (Hanover, Mass.: Maple Street Press, 2010), p. 72.
50 Lyons sat in his first . . . winning football games.: Scott, p. 139.
50 Along the way, Lyons . . . good things would happen.: Scott, p. 139.
51 his mind was on . . . well, you watch,": Scott, p. 52.
52 "We just knew we were going to win,": Todd Jones, "Run for the Roses," *Yea Alabama 2009*, p. 43.
53 "It felt like a funeral,": Steve Kirk, "Dead Just a Month Ago, Tide Revives, *The Birmingham News*, Feb. 11, 2006, p. 6-B.
54 Bear Bryant figured it . . . since he had cried.: Gold, p. 197.
54 In 1965, a writer . . . went to Texas A&M.": Gold, p. 197.

54 Bear Bryant said, he . . . he was losing him.: Gold, p. 197.
55 Growing up, his family . . . with his savior.: Scott, pp. 166-67.
56 The Tide sports information . . . known as the Italian Stallion.: Scott, pp. 121-22.
57 As the first half . . . SEC games at home.: Bolton, *The Basketball Tide*, pp. 98-99.
58 "Our defensive line is going . . . you can get whipped.": Austin Murphy, "The Tide Is Turning," *Sports Illustrated*, Sept. 8, 2008, http://www.sportsillustrated.cnn.com/vault/article/magazine/MAG1144910/index.htm.
59 when halfback Dixie Howell . . . bomb for a touchdown.: Gold, p. 59.
60 The game was supposed . . . that had failed.: Doug Segrest, "The Night the Tide Put College Ball on TV," *The Birmingham News*, Oct. 9, 2009, p. 1-C.
61 When he left his . . . see his car again.: Ray Melick, "Thompson to Fine-Tune His Game," *The Birmingham News*, Sept. 2, 2007, p. 15-C.
61 It's been a wild ride,": Melick, "Thompson to Fine-Tune His Game."
62 In Sept. 1995 Jackson . . . of kidney problems.: Doug Segrest, "Jackson Was Gone," *The Birmingham News*, Sept. 17, 1996, p. 01-C.
63 In 1961, it became official. Bear Bryant was a prophet.": Gold, p. 99.
63 the first meeting . . . would be national champions.: Gold, p. 99.
63 Billy Neighbors said he thought the man was crazy.: Scott, p. 82.
64 After Alabama upset . . . a monster game now.": Steve Irvine, "Bigger Than Shoes," *The Birmingham News*, March 25, 2004, p. 1-B.
65 Don't go! Don't go in there!" . . . same way Booth had: Wade, p. 136.
66 The head coach finally . . . to reach 100 points.: Bolton, *The Basketball Tide*, p. 107.
67 The reporters in Arizona couldn't believe it,": Steve Kirk, "Tide Pride Showing in World Series Debut," *The Birmingham News*, May 25, 2001, p. 01-D.
68 Steve Sloan was minding . . . for the Sugar Bowl.: Hicks, p. 36.
68 When the starter got . . . quarterback would start.; Hicks, p. 36.
68 the coaches forgot that . . . the whole first half.: Hicks, pp. 38-49.
69 "It wasn't going to . . . We had a hunger.": Bill Bryant, "After Stewing for a Year, Tide Gets Revenge," *The Huntsville Times*, Dec. 6, 2009, http://www.al.com/sports/huntsvilletimes/bbryant.ssf?base/sports.

SOURCES

"#2 Alabama 20 -- #22 South Carolina 6." *Yea Alabama*. Hanover, Mass.: Maple Street Press LLC, 2010.
"Bear Bryant Knew How to Be Nice." *Redelephants.com*. http://www.red elephants.com/CoachBearBryant.html.
Beech, Mark. "The Tide Has Turned." *Sports Illustrated*. 10 Oct. 2005. http://www.sportsillustrated.cnn.com/vault/article/magazine/MAG1103865/index.htm.
"Blind Golfer 'Reads' the Greens." *The Palm Beach Post*. 1 March 1971. http://www.news.google.com/newspapers?nid=1964&dat=19710301.
Bolton, Clyde. *The Basketball Tide*. Huntsville: The Strode Publishers, 1977.
-----. *The Crimson Tide*. Huntsville: The Strode Publishers, 1972.
Browning, Al. Third Saturday in October: *The Game-by Game Story of the South's Most Intense Football Rivalry*. Nashville: Cumberland House Publishing, 2001.
Bryant, Bill. "After Stewing for a Year, Tide Gets Revenge." *The Huntsville Times*. 6 Dec. 2009. http://www.al.com/sports/huntsvilletimes/bbryant.ssf?base/sports.
"Charles A. Boswell." *Encyclopedia of Alabama*. http://www.encyclopediaof alabama.org/face/Article.jsp?id=h-1771.
Deford, Frank. "I Do Love the Football." Sports Illustrated. 23 Nov. 1981. http://www.sportsillustrated.cnn.com/vault/article/magazine/MAG1125024/index.html.
Estes, Genry. "Hope Is Alive." *The Mobile Press-Register*. 31 May 2009. http://www.al.com/alabamabaseball/mobileregister/women.ssf?/base/sports.
Gold, Eli. *Crimson Nation*. Nashville: Rutledge Hill Press, 2005.
Hicks, Tommy. *Game of My Life: Alabama: Memorable Stories of Crimson Tide Football*. Champaign, Il.: Sports Publishing, L.L.C., 2006.
Holiday, Pete. "On the Mark. 'Bama Wins Championships and Now Heismans." *Yea Alabama 2009*. Hanover, Mass.: Maple Street Press LLC, 2010. 71-76.
Irvine, Steve. "Bigger Than Shoes." *The Birmingham News*. 25 March 2004. 1-B.
-----. "One Is Done." *The Birmingham News*. 21 March 2004. 1-C.
"Joe Namath." *Wikipedia, the free encyclopedia*. http://www.en.wikipedia.org/wiki/Joe_Namath.
Jones, Todd. "Run for the Roses." *Yea Alabama 2009*. Hanover, Mass.: Maple Street Press LLC, 2010. 17-69.
Kennedy, Ray. "Battle for Braggin' Rights." *Sports Illustrated*. 9 Dec. 1974. http://www/sportsillustrated.cnn.com/vault/article/magazine/MAG 1089323/index.htm.
Kirk, Steve. "Dead Just a Month Ago, Tide Revives." *The Birmingham News*. 11 Feb. 2006. 6-B.
-----. "Not Like They Drew It Up." *The Birmingham News*. 25 Sept. 2005. 1-C.
-----. "Tide Coach Embraces Slap-Hitting Speedster: Hug Convinces Rogers She Belonged on Team." *The Birmingham News*. 10 May 2006. 1-C.
-----. "Tide Pride Showing in World Series Debut." *The Birmingham News*. 25 May 25 2001. 01-D.

Crimson Tide

Kirkpatrick, Curry. "Solution to a Thorny Problem." *Sports Illustrated*. 15 March 1982. http://www.sportsillustrated.cnn.com/vault/article/magazine/MAG1125307/index.htm.

Kirshenbaum, Herry. "High Tide Washes over Vols." *Sports Illustrated*. 13 Feb. 1978. http://www.sportsillustrated.cnn.com/vault/article/magazine/MAG1093316/index.htm.

Lake, Thomas. "The Shot That Saved Lives." *Sports Illustrated*. 16 March 2009. http://www.sportsillustrated.cnn.com/vault/article/magazine/MAG153064/index.htm.

Melick, Ray. "A Serious Miler." *The Birmingham News*. 28 May 2009. 1-C.

-----. "Thompson to Fine-Tune His Game." *The Birmingham News*. 2 Sept. 2007, 15-C.

Murphy, Austin. "A Tidy Finish." *Sports Illustrated*. 14 Dec. 1992. http://www/sportsillustrated.cnn.com/vault/article/magazine/MAG1004647/index.htm.

-----. "The Tide Is Turning." *Sports Illustrated*. 8 Sept. 2008. http://www.sportsillustrated.cnn.com/vault/article/magazine/MAG1144910/index.htm.

Puma, Mike. "Bear Bryant 'Simply the Best There Ever Was.'" *ESPN*. http://espn.go.com/classic/biography/s/Bryant_Bear.html.

Rapaport, Ian R. "Apologetic Wells Returns as Coach." *The Birmingham News*. 28 June 2007. 1-B.

-----. "Turning Points: Changes Started During Practices for Bowl Game." *The Birmingham News*. 2 Dec. 2008. 1-C.

Rhoden, William C. "Dareus's Big Plays Surprised Even Him." *The New York Times*. 8 Jan. 2010. http://www.nytimes.com/2010/01/09/sports/ncaafootball/09rhoden.html.

Scott, Richard. *Legends of Alabama Football*. Champaign, IL.: Sports Publishing L.L.C., 2004.

Segrest, Doug. "Bama Sacks Michigan." The Birmingham News. 2 Jan. 1997. 01-C.

-----. "Jackson Was Gone." *The Birmingham News*. 17 Sept. 17 1996. 01-C.

-----. "Raising the Bar." *The Birmingham News*. 5 March 2003. 1-D.

-----. "The Night the Tide Put College Ball on TV." *The Birmingham News*. 9 Oct. 2009. 1-C.

Wade, Don. *Always Alabama: A History of Crimson Tide Football*. New York: Simon & Schuster, 2006.

Wojciechowski, Gene. "Tide at Pinnacle of College Football." *ESPN.com*. 7 Jan. 2013. http://www.espn.go.com/college-football/bowls.